I0170396

George S. Patton, Jr.
And
Ranulf Compton

War Diary
1918

DALE STREET BOOKS
Silver Spring, Maryland

America was the great hope of France and England. It was the American troops which, already in July, 1918, had covered the roads to Paris and which now, in the autumn of 1918, formed the great reserve for Marshal Foch's offensive which, without this American help, was absolutely not feasible. This help was therefore, from the moral, material and operative point of view, of the greatest importance.

The American soldier went into battle in the first enthusiasm of war, which had long since become an earnest conception of duty with Germans, English and French, and in an ignorance of the horrors of modern methods of warfare. While the Frenchman and Englishman began an assault only from well-prepared fields of attack, after an artillery preparation lasting several hours and preceded by battalions of tanks, and while their assaults came to an immediate stop when those means of attack broke down, the American soldier knew as yet no fear of losses. He could be placed anywhere and he could be sent forward from wholly unprepared fields of attack, as was done east of the Argonne. This novice willingly accepted the hardest losses as something quite natural, just as every German, Englishman and Frenchman, and every gallant soldier had done and would have done at the beginning of the war.

Major Hermann von Giehrl,
Battle of the Meuse-Argonne from the German Perspective
(Silver Spring, MD: Dale Street Books, 2017), p. 51.

All Tank Corps photographs by U.S. Army Signal Corps.
All diary images and cover design by Aleksandra M. Rohde.

Copyright © 2018 by Aleksandra M. Rohde
All rights reserved.

TABLE OF CONTENTS

Illustrations

PREFACE

George S. Patton, Jr., maintained an official war diary while he commanded the 304th (1st Provisional) Tank Brigade of the American Expeditionary Forces in 1918 France. It is published for the first time in <u>War Diary 1918</u>, along with the war diary of Ranulf Compton. Compton, one of Patton's battalion commanders, assumed command of all brigade tanks at the front after Patton was wounded the first day of the Meuse-Argonne Offensive—and with some of the fiercest fighting still ahead.

Patton's brigade diary is valuable for its daily history covering the two great battles led by Americans under General John J. Pershing, Commander of the A.E.F.; the Battle of St. Mihiel and the Meuse-Argonne Offensive. However, Patton's diary does not contain the level of detail—or the candid observations—of the war diary kept by Captain Compton; particularly since Compton led the brigade tank crews into some of their toughest combat.

As an early proponent of tanks, it is understandable that Patton might possess a certain reluctance to cast too harsh a light on the problems of early tank warfare. Compton's eyewitness reports from the front suffered from no such political veneer—with history buffs and military scholars the luckier for it.

I discovered these war diaries during a weeks-long road trip visiting various archives in search of rare Patton documents. Having already visited the Ft. Riley Museum and the Eisenhower Presidential Library in Kansas, next on the agenda was the Chester Fritz Library at the University of North Dakota—more specifically its Orin G. Libby Manuscript Collection which includes "George S. Patton Papers, 1918-1944."

The Patton Papers are stored on the library's second floor in a large, airy room furnished with sturdy wooden tables and good lighting. Placing my request with the cheerful librarian at the front desk (who wanted to know how I had even heard of the collection), I took my seat next to a large window looking out onto the windswept Dakota landscape.

It was not long before an archival storage box filled with numbered manila folders was placed on my table. I pulled out the first folder—1360-1—and turned back its cover.

Tucked inside was a thin, yellowed booklet. Preprinted on the cover was a list of 10 items titled, "War Diary Instructions." Penned in cursive at the upper right corner was "August 1918." Below it was written "345th Battalion" and below that, "304th (1st) Brigade Tank Corps."

The diary was signed in the bottom right corner by someone at that time unfamiliar to me—Ranulf Compton. According to his signature block, he was a captain in the Tank Corps and also the commander of the 345th Battalion. The booklet pages were formatted for daily entries. Every day's entry was handwritten and signed by Compton.

Each numbered manila folder held one such booklet and each booklet contained one month of daily entries. August, September and October diaries for the 345th Battalion were filed in folders 1360-1, 1360-2 and 1360-3 respectively.

Inside folder 1360-4, I found a war diary for September 1918. Written at the top right corner was "304th (1st Brigade) Tank Corps." The cover and daily entries were signed by "G.S. Patton, Jr., Col. T.C." Folders 1360-5 to 1360-9 contained the 304th Brigade war diaries for October 1918 to February 1919. All were signed by Patton.

My journey was well rewarded. It was the culmination of both lucky circumstances and some investigative research that began with another trip the previous April to Carlisle, Pennsylvania.

Carlisle is the home of the U.S. Army Heritage and Education Center. Located adjacent to the Army War College, it is a major repository for rare military records. I went there in search of an early report written by Patton in November 1918, "304th American Brigade at St. Mihiel." Patton's report was appended to a larger report compiled by Brigadier General Samuel D. Rockenbach in November 1918 titled U.S. Army Expeditionary Force, France, 1917-1919, Tank Corps: Report Operations Tank Corps, A.E.F. , and commonly referred to as "the Rockenbach Report."[1]

By the time the Americans entered the Great War in the latter part of 1917 the British and French had already developed their own versions of the new inventions called tanks. If the Americans were to be a credible ally, they would have to quickly design, manufacture and field tanks of their own. General Pershing chose Samuel Rockenbach to lead that effort.

The Rockenbach Report documented the birth and growth of the Tank Corps from the first decisions on tank design and manufacture, to the development of tactics, organization, assignment of personnel, training; and finally to the delivery of the heavy beasts into wartime France where they would be tested in the heat of battle.

In addition to Patton's report on St. Mihiel another supporting document, "1st (304th) American Brigade at Meuse-Argonne," also intrigued me. It was written by Major

[1] Samuel D. Rockenbach, Operations of the Tank Corps, A.E.F. (Silver Spring: Dale Street Books, 2017). Verbatim transcript of original report by Samuel D. Rockenbach, U.S. Army Expeditionary Force, France, 1917-1919, Tank Corps: Report Operations Tank Corps, A.E.F. (France: General HQs A.E.F., Office of Chief of Tank Corps, 1918), Carlisle: U.S. Army Heritage and Education Center, Ridgway Hall, D608.U56 1918.

Sereno E. Brett. As with Ranulf Compton initially, this was a new name to me.

In searching through the documents I learned that Patton's tank brigade consisted of two American tank battalions (in addition to a group of French tanks)— the 344th commanded by Major Brett and the 345th by Captain Compton. After Patton was wounded, Brett assumed command of the brigade. Compton was placed in command of all the brigade tanks at the front.

Initially working for Patton and then assuming command of his brigade, Patton-related documents likely crossed Brett's desk on a regular basis. Luckily for historians, he retained and preserved boxes of these records. An Internet search of Sereno E. Brett led me to the Chester Fritz Library, the recipient of his considerable largesse, including Patton's and Compton's war diaries.

Reproduced here are Patton's diaries covering the months from September 1918 to the cessation of hostilities in November and Compton's diaries from mid-August 1918 to the end of October. Oddly, Brett's official war diaries were not included with the archived collection. However, daily entries pertaining to Brett's battalion were entered into Patton's brigade diary, presumably taken from Brett's war diary entries.

Some explanation about the origin and purpose of the war diaries might be helpful at this point to better understand their significance and how they were administered.

To create an official record of the American involvement in the Great War, the War Department required commanders "at battalion and higher" to keep a daily diary of operations—i.e., a "war diary." A regulation was published listing types of information to be recorded in the diary, including "a march table, or statement of operations

viii

or location of the organization, including an account of weather, roads, camp, health of troops, etc.," and "followed by a chronological record of events..."[2]

The regulation also required "each day's record...be forwarded daily to the next higher commander, who, as soon as practicable after the receipt thereof, will forward the war diary direct to the War Department."[3]

Preprinted booklets formatted to insure compliance with the regulation were distributed to the commands. Unlike the War Department regulation, the booklets contained instructions that they were to be returned completed "at the end of each calendar month." Either way, the record was to be approved by the commander or his adjutant and signed by the commander before forwarding ultimately to the War Department for compilation into an official history of the war.

Here is the full list of ten "War Diary Instructions" printed on the cover of every booklet:

1. *Observe F.S.R., [Field Service Regulations], para. 35.*
2. *This is the HISTORY of what your unit accomplishes, in other words, of OPERATIONS. Tell what actually happened; not what is supposed to have happened. Abstain from criticism.*
3. *Append all orders, messages, plans, sketches, etc.*
4. *Designate precisely each place and position occupied; assume that the reader never heard of any of them.*
5. *Note the personnel, losses and statistics of unit as changes occur; give dates, hours, state of weather, atmosphere and roads.*

---

[2] Field Service Regulations United States Army 1914, corrected to July 31, 1918, para. 35 (Washington: War Department, 1918), p. 22.

[3] The reason we assume Sereno Brett's battalion war diary was incorporated into Patton's brigade war diary.

6. *Enter the higher units to which you belong; brigades, divisions, corps, etc.*
7. *When maneuvering, always try to get the designations and positions of units next to you in line.*
8. *Tactical observations are particularly desired.*
9. *No erasures may be made in the Diary.*
10. *The C.O. must sign before the return is made at the end of the calendar month.*

Inside the booklets, preprinted headings were followed by blank spaces to record information regarding troop movements, personnel available for duty, weather, roads, health, camp, casualties, captures, and a report ("narrative") on operations. On the next page is an image Patton's war diary for September 1, 1918. As is evident from the image, he did not fill in all the blanks requesting information.

For September 1, Patton filled in the blanks pertaining to numbers of officers and men available for duty, condition of the weather, and roads. He did not enter information on other requested items, such as the march table, general health, and condition of the camp for that day. Further, different blanks were filled in by both Patton and Compton in their diaries for different days, depending on the circumstances. For instance, there was no need to report on casualties and losses when the units were not in combat; or on the march table when units were not deployed.

Accordingly, the type of information included at the top of each transcribed page in this book will vary depending on what was originally entered into the diary for that day.

Image of George S. Patton, Jr.'s September 1, 1918 entry in his brigade War Diary.

As required by regulation, Patton appended (usually glued) into the booklets "orders, messages, plans, sketches, etc.," adjacent to the relevant diary entries. As with the diary entries, these appended documents are transcribed verbatim here, excluding only minor administration details such as distribution lists and typist's initials.

To help distinguish between the written entry and these appended documents, a line is drawn above and below the appended documents and a different font used to further distinguish between the two. (Compton did not affix relevant documents to the pages of his diary, unfortunately. In a letter to Patton, Compton mentioned keeping his relevant documents in a separate file.[4] However this file was not found in the library collection.)

On some diary pages, references to maps were written in the left margin. These are transcribed and inserted above the narrative of operations. On other pages only the day of the week (i.e., Sunday, Monday, etc.) was written into the margin. These marginal entries are not included in the transcript, unless the day of the week was accompanied by other details, such as map information. While no maps were found accompanying the archived diaries, map references are retained for their historical significance.

Minor formatting and editorial changes have been made for consistency or clarity. Obvious spelling and minor grammatical errors have been corrected whenever possible rather than using the notation [sic], which is used only sparingly. When there is ambiguity or another unique circumstance, an explanation or additional information is provided in the footnotes.

---

[4] See memo preceding diary entry for August 21, 1918, "345th (327th) Battalion, August 1918."

Where locations were written in French (e.g., "Bois," "Ferme" or "Saillant") the French is retained for this transcription (but without the accent marks since these were largely excluded in the original entries). Where the location was written in its English translation, the English version is transcribed (e.g., "Woods," "Farm" or "Salient,"). There are some instances where the Anglicized version of a name differs significantly from the French version. In those instances, the French version is footnoted.

The locations referenced in this diary are important not only for their historical significance but as reminders of war's toll in human suffering. Some of the villages and farms were reduced to rubble and never rebuilt. Many of the temporary military structures such as the infamous trenches were dismantled after the war. These places deserve to be remembered. That begins by correctly spelling their names.

Our mission at Dale Street Books is to rediscover and preserve history that might otherwise be forgotten. In addition to publishing books that are free of aging imperfections, and therefore easier to read, we take care to correctly identify (and correctly spell) the names of people and places. We do this by retyping the original document into a word file, using JPEG images we take of the original as reference.

Some words are so faded the only thing left is the shadow created where the typewriter key punched through the paper many years ago. By enlarging the JPEG image we oftentimes can decipher the word, literally from its shadow. We crop and enhance the images of any accompanying photographs, charts, diagrams, etc., and insert them into the word file as they were positioned in the original layout. Sometimes words in the original text are faded AND misspelled, making our research that much more challenging.

When we first began reproducing old documents, we naively thought we could simply check the standard references pertaining to the era to find the correct spellings. Instead, frequently what we found were inconsistent spellings of the same name–or could not find the name at all. There are likely a couple of reasons for this.

First of all, how a name is spelled in a secondary source depends in large part on which primary source was referenced—and the spelling acumen (or not) of its author. The original U.S. Army reports, memorandums, war diaries, etc., were written by Americans who were not necessarily fluent in French. Even Patton who professed a fluency in the language was a notoriously poor speller, even in his native tongue. So it should be no surprise that military reports might contain misspellings of French locations. One could easily imagine as many possible combinations in the spelling of a name as there were primary sources referencing it.

Second of all, the Great War took place in a time before mass communications, the computer and the Internet. Today we take for granted that events are thoroughly reported and recorded. Not so one hundred years ago. Some of the places referenced in the old military reports were destroyed in the war leaving behind little or no record of their prior existence. Unless captured in some enduring format of the time (e.g., photographs, reports, personal letters or newspaper accounts) they could easily be lost to recorded history as memories faded and died.

To help us find historically obscure places, we learned to rely on a number of credible resources, beginning with the invaluable network of regional and national archives and libraries.

The National Archives located in College Park, Maryland is the home to millions of historical government (including military) documents, photographs and images dating back to the early 1700's. What you do not find there you might discover at the U.S. Army Heritage and Education Center, located in Carlisle, Pennsylvania.

By example, the National Archives does not have a copy of the Rockenbach Report, which is the seminal work on the early Tank Corps. The Army Heritage and Education Center holds two copies; one with the main report and most of the accompanying addendums and one with just the main report.

The Eisenhower Presidential Library, located in Abilene, Kansas, has an entire Patton collection. Especially interesting are the letters from Patton to Eisenhower regarding the "slapping incident" and Patton's resistance to de-Nazification after the war in 1945.

Fort Riley, down the road from Abilene, while not as well funded as the larger archives and libraries, does maintain a small repository of Army journals and publications dating back to the 1800's and including the time of Patton's tour of duty at Ft. Riley's Mounted Service School in 1913 and 1914.

The manuscript collection at the Chester Fritz Library may seem a distant location for such an important repository; but it is a world class operation storing some of the most complete documents related to the Tank Corps in World War I. This library maintains a copy of the Rockenbach Report with more of the original addendums attached and in better condition than even the copies of the Report stored at the Army Heritage and Education Center. Of course, it is also home to the original handwritten war diaries for George S. Patton, Jr. and Ranulf Compton.

The internet has also been a tremendous resource in helping locate reference materials as well as check on possible spelling variations. Wikipedia pages have been especially helpful with locating old French landmarks, such as villages and chateaus. While we do not rely solely on the internet, it is an invaluable tool to help locate additional sources and to corroborate spellings we find cited elsewhere.

Our research experiences also led us to several publications that we found especially informative and reliable. One immensely helpful resource for this book was volume 2 of the <u>Order of Battle of the United States Land Forces in the World War – American Expeditionary Forces: Divisions</u>, which details by dates and locations the movements of American Divisions in 1917 and 1918.[5]

General Pershing's Memoirs, <u>My Experiences in the World War</u>[6] and Collier's Encyclopedia , <u>The Story of the Great War</u> (especially volume XV),[7] were also very informative.

Still, there were a few times we were left scratching our heads. Either no reference could be found, or several respected sources spelled names in different ways. In those instances we provide a footnote to address the ambiguity.

Within the war diary there were also a few individuals who had several variations on the spelling of their names; or more commonly, they were cited using only their last names. Whenever the surname only was provided in the diary, the full name is footnoted at first use. Reference for

[5] <u>Order of Battle of the United States Land Forces in the World War</u>, Vol. 2, "American Expeditionary Forces: Divisions " (Washington, D.C.: Center of Military History United States Army, 1988).

[6] John J. Pershing, <u>My Experiences in the World War</u>, Vols. I and II (New York: Frederick A. Stokes Company, 1931).

[7] <u>The Story of the Great War</u>, Vol. XV (New York: P. F. Collier & Son, 1920).

officers' full names is the manning document dated September 10, 1918, "Organization Tank Corps 1st Army," appended to the Rockenbach Report.[8]

This manning document did not include names of enlisted men. However, the brigade diary for October 2, 1918 listed the names of enlisted men receiving temporary officer appointments. Also, a list of approximately 150 officers and enlisted men (with serial numbers) assigned to the Provisional Company, 1st Brigade, was affixed to the pages between the October 13 and 14 brigade diary entries. Both these lists are reproduced in full here.

The September 10th manning document also listed Patton's Tank Brigade as the "1st Brigade American." It had been originally designated the 304th in August 1918 and redesignated the "1st Provisional" shortly thereafter.[9] But some of the diary pages for September and October still listed the brigade as the 304th.

Adding to the confusion, the brigade was redesignated back to the 304th in November 1918.[10] The manning document listed the two American battalions in the brigade as the 326th and the 327th. They were redesignated on September 12, 1918 to the 344th and 345th respectively.[11]

Abbreviations were commonly used in the war diary entries. When abbreviations might be unfamiliar to the reader, they have been spelled out in at least the first use. Abbreviations in appended documents remain as they appear in the originals.

[8] Rockenbach, pp. 77-82.

[9] Robert E. Rogge, "304th Tank Brigade: Its Formation and First Two Actions," Armor, Vol. XCVII, No. 4 (July-August 1988), pp. 26-34.

[10] Order of Battle of the United States Land Forces in the World War (1917-1919): Vol. Three, Part 2, "Directory of Troops" (Washington: U.S. Government Printing Office, 1949), p. 1543.

[11] 304th (1st) Brigade War Diary entry for September 12.

It appears to have been the stylistic protocol to capitalize all letters in names of geographic locations. This device has been retained as in the original.

The accepted convention on numbering units—Roman numerals for corps level (e.g., V Corps rather than Fifth Corps or 5th Corps) and armies spelled out (First Army rather than 1st Army)—was not applied in the diary entries. The entries have not been corrected to adhere to convention, but reproduced as they were originally written.

Inspecting the handwritten copy of Patton's diary, it is evident that Patton wrote the first nine days of diary entries (September 1 to 9) in his own hand. His signature matches the body of the text—and his hurried penmanship style is distinct in its near illegibility. A sudden change to a neater, more legible, handwriting on September 10 indicates Patton delegated the task of recording the entries to someone else beginning on that date. However, on some of the entries written after the 10th, comments continued to be added or corrections made in Patton's distinctive script.

See the following example of Patton's unique penmanship on display, adding a comment to the day's entry.

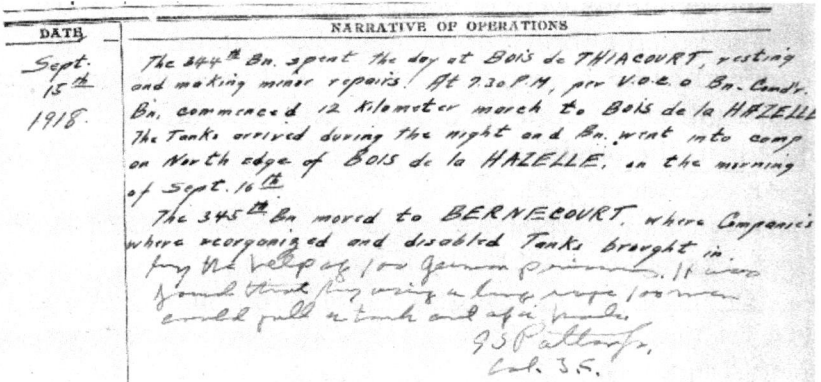

Image of Patton's September 15, 1918 entry in his brigade War Diary.

The entries written in Patton's own hand (including the entire entries for the first nine days) are reproduced in italics in this book. Beginning September 10, the few comments and corrections obviously in his handwriting are bolded as well as italicized for ease of identification within the text.

Every entry, except for two, was personally signed by Patton for the duration of the war, even during the period Brett had assumed command of the brigade and for at least several months after the war ended. This seems to indicate that not all responsibility for the brigade had passed to Brett.

The September 4 diary entry for the brigade is unsigned, most likely inadvertently. The diary entry for September 26, the day Patton was wounded, is also understandably unsigned. Because all the entries but two were signed, the signatures have not been transcribed to avoid redundancy and preserve space in the transcribed text.

Ranulf Compton possessed handwriting as distinctive as Patton's, except it was uniformly neat with a signature punctuated by elegant flourishes.

Image of Ranulf Compton's September 13, 1918 entry in his battalion War Diary.

Compton also signed each day's diary entries. But where Patton passed the job of scribing daily entries to someone else after September 10 (albeit continuing to review and sign each day); Compton personally wrote all his own diary entries. (His signature block also is not transcribed here to avoid redundancy and preserve space.)

Patton's and Compton's war diaries, so rich in operational, logistical and personnel detail, add considerably to the body of knowledge related to the early Tank Corps and its deployment into wartime France. War Diary 1918, the verbatim transcription of these one-of-a-kind handwritten war diaries, makes this rich historical detail now widely accessible.

War Diary 1918 also helps to bestow, at long last, well-deserved recognition on Ranulf Compton. He may not have been a favorite of Patton's, but by an irony of fate, he would go on to lead the frontline units of Patton's beloved Tank Brigade into some of the toughest fighting of the war. To grateful historians everywhere, he would also leave behind a candid account of how tanks fared in that fighting.

Aleksandra Miesak Rohde
April 2018

INTRODUCTION

The tank is a temperamental beast which has been slowly trained to routine; but he is a fiery dragon of wrath when loosed in the enemy's country. Tanks had been seen trundling about ahead of the infantry across roads, fields, trenches, ditches, looking for machine-gun nests which they might devour.[1]

The United States declared war on Germany and Austria-Hungary in 1917, joining the French and British Empire in what was called The Great War. By then, the war had already been raging three long years. Adversaries on both sides had become seasoned fighters, armed with the latest advancements in aircraft, heavy artillery, poison gas and mortars. The war's modern weaponry was perhaps best epitomized by the tank, an armored vehicle with explosive firepower, capable of tearing through the ubiquitous barbed wire and withstanding the withering machine gun fire.

By the middle of 1918 the American Expeditionary Forces, over a million fighting men commanded by General John J. Pershing, would arrive in Europe to fight alongside their allies. There was only a year to prepare and there was much work to do. Along with raising the necessary forces, the Americans would have to equip for the modern battlefield—including tanks, which were not at that time part of the American arsenal.

Prior to the arrival of the A.E.F., the American Military Mission in Paris had, by direction of the Chief of the War College, investigated and submitted a report under date of May 21st, 1917, giving the latest British and French technical and tactical ideas on the use of Tanks. Major Frank Parker, Liaison Officer at G.H.Q. of the French Armies of the North and North-East, submitted notes covering French Tanks in the Allied Offensive of April,

---

[1] Frederick Palmer, <u>American in France</u> (New York: Dodd, Mead and Company, 1918), p. 431.

1917. In the light of our recent experience his two chief criticisms are of interest:

> *"(a) Insufficient protection against fire. Little extinguishing material was provided.*
> *(b) Faulty liaison with the Infantry. On several occasions the Tanks went ahead of the Infantry and were destroyed for lack of support. Many were destroyed."[2]*

The British and French had already been developing different types of tanks. The British preferred a heavy tank, while the French, a lighter model. The Americans were unsure what type of tank they should acquire. There was also the question of tactics.

A joint British and French Tank Board met in London early in May [1917], but were unable to reconcile their ideas as to machines or tactics. The British preferred the heavy Tank to be used in advance of the Infantry and the French desired their light Tank, which they were building, to be used in close liaison with the Infantry.[3]

In the end, the Americans decided on a mix of heavy and light tanks.

The best British heavy Tank at that time, the Mark IV, has been aptly described as a deaf, dumb, and blind beast. An improvement had to be made on that, and as far as we could get any consensus of opinion, the Liberty or Mark VIII would possess all the qualities that the fighting man requires. The United States could not manufacture guns and armor plate in time to be of any use. If we got heavy Tanks, it would have to be an Anglo-American machine.

---

[2] Rockenbach, p. 12.
[3] Rockenbach, p. 13.

For the light Tank, the French Renault was decided on, but with a number of essential improvements. It was to have a bulkhead separating the gun room from the engine so that the crew could not be burned to death; was to have a self-starter; was to have its gasoline Tank double cased with an inch of felt lining between, so that when penetrated by a bullet there would be no leakage of gas; and to have an interchangeable mount so that the same Tank could carry either a machine gun or a 37mm gun.[4]

Driver opens window in machine gun tank.
Tank Corps School near Langres, France, July 15, 1918.

The American effort to acquire tanks was amply validated by the Battle of Cambrai, a British attack to break through the German defences on the Cambrai front.

At 6.20 a.m. on the 20th November [1917], without any previous artillery bombardment, tanks and infantry attacked on a front of about six miles from east of

[4] Rockenbach, pp. 16, 17.

Gonnelieu to the Canal du Nord opposite Hermies...On the
principal front of attack, the tanks moved forward in
advance of the infantry, crushing down the enemy's wire
and forming great lanes through which our infantry could
pass. Protected by smoke barrages from the view of the
enemy's artillery, they rolled on across the German
trenches, smashing up the enemy's machine guns and
driving his infantry to ground. Close behind our tanks our
own infantry followed and, while the tanks patrolled the
line of hostile trenches, cleared the German infantry from
their dug-outs and shelters. In this way, both the main
system of the Hindenburg Line and its outer defences
were rapidly over-run, and tanks and infantry proceeded
in accordance with programme to attack upon the
Hindenburg Reserve Line...[5]

Earlier that November George S. Patton, Jr. had already
been detailed to run the American Tank School and Center
for light (Renault) tanks, to be established near Langres,
France. (Diary entries refer variously to Brennes, Bourg and
Langres as the site of the Tank Center. They are all in the
same location; Langres being the town and Brennes and
Bourg two small villages close by.)

The Renault, equipped with a four-cylinder gasoline
engine could travel between 1 and 5 miles per hour
depending on conditions. "The heaviest armor was only
16mm thick, proof against machine gun bullets and shell
splinters... The driver was in front, and the commander
stood in the turret. Crew communication was by yelling and
kicks from the commander's foot."[6]

General Pershing appointed Colonel Samuel D.
Rockenbach, Chief of the Tank Corps in December 1917.
(Rockenbach was promoted to Brigadier General in July
1918.)[7] Rockenbach had a difficult mission ahead of him.

[5] J. H. Boraston, Ed., <u>Sir Douglas Haig's Despatches</u> (London &
Toronto: J. M. Dent & Sons Ltd., 1919), p. 154.

[6] Rogge, p. 27.

[7] Martin Blumenson, <u>The Patton Papers 1885-1940</u> (Boston: Houghton

INTRODUCTION

He would have to solve basic questions of tactics, design, and organization before he could even plan for deployment into the European battlefield—and the clock was ticking as forces were hurriedly assembled for the overseas mission.

By late August 1918 plans were underway for an operation at St. Mihiel early the next month. Lieutenant Colonel Patton was now in command of the 304th Tank Brigade. In addition to an attachment of French tank units, the 304th Brigade contained two American tank battalions, both operating with the Renault light tanks; the 326th, commanded by Major Sereno E. Brett and the 327th, commanded by Captain Ranulf Compton. Patton was busy preparing for combat. He had waited for this moment and would soon get his chance, first at the Battle of St. Mihiel and then the Meuse-Argonne Offensive. But it did not turn out as he might have anticipated.

Mifflin Company, 1972), p. 550.

Lieutenant Colonel George S. Patton, Jr. in command of the first Tank Center. Tank Corps School near Langres, France, July 15, 1918.

Left to Right – Sergeant Casey, Captain Ranulf Compton, Sergeant Holliday, Tank Corps School near Langres, France, July 15, 1918.

Left to Right – Captain Williams, Major Sereno E. Brett, Captain Ranulf Compton near Langres, France, July 15, 1918.

Just as the War Department was deliberately planning for deployment into the European theatre, it was just as deliberately planning to capture the history and lessons learned there. Accordingly, a regulation was issued requiring all commanders, battalion and up, as part of their official duties, to keep a war diary.

> *A war diary is a record of events kept in campaign by each battalion and higher organization, each ammunition, supply, engineer, and sanitary train. Entries are made daily and should form a concise history of the military operations...Each day's record will commence with a march table, or statement of the operations or location of the organization, including an account of weather, roads, camp, health of troops, etc., and a statement of the supply of ammunition, rations, and forage. This will be followed by a chronological record of events, including time and place of issue and receipt of orders and messages, with a copy of a synopsis of contents. It is of special importance that the exact hour and place at which movements are begun and ended, and orders or important messages sent or received, be noted. After an engagement, the war diary will contain a report of losses and captures...* [8]

Consistent with the War Department's mandate, Patton was responsible for keeping the brigade diary and each of his battalion commanders for keeping his own. The subordinate commanders were to forward their diaries to the higher headquarters who would send them on to the War Department.

These war diaries were official records and no place for colorful—i.e., blunt—expressions of personal views, unlike what scholars have found in the pages of Patton's personal diary and letters home to his wife Beatrice. His personal diary and letters home have been studied extensively and referenced in scholarly works by respected authors such as Martin Blumenson and Stanley P. Hirshson. The war diary is less well known and therefore intriguing for additional insights revealed in Patton's brigade diary and more so in

---

[8] <u>Field Service Regulations United States Army 1914</u>, para. 35, p. 22.

the diary of one of his battalion commanders, Captain Compton.

In the early weeks of September, Compton's daily battalion diary entries were perfunctory, brief references to inspections conducted, schools attended, ammunition issued and equipment tested. Consistent with the regulation requiring subordinate commanders to forward their daily entries to the next higher command, it was not surprising that his early entries were incorporated, often verbatim, into Patton's brigade diary. (Sereno Brett's diary was not found with the Patton and Compton diary collection. But it is fair to assume that his diary entries were likewise incorporated into the brigade war diary.)

But once combat operations began, first at the Battle of St. Mihiel on September 12 and then beginning on September 26 for the Meuse-Argonne Offensive, the nature of the diary entries changed. Instead of the formerly brief remarks, Compton's entries now consumed multiple pages with details evoking the chaos of battle fought in the miserable rain and impenetrable fog against an intransigent enemy fully armed with artillery, machine guns, and gas—and with tanks that proved disastrously vulnerable to the mud, trenches, shell holes, short supplies of petrol, and their own mechanical shortcomings. Below is part of Compton's war diary entry for September 12:

> ...At 5:00 a.m., the official "H" hour, the tanks took off with the infantry. At 9:00 a.m. the Battalion Commander reported:
> 25 tanks engaged
> 11 tanks disabled in action
> 10 disabled at or near P.D.[9]
> 3 going into action
> 7 supply tanks
> 56 total
> 16 brigade reserve
> 72 total battalion tanks

[9] Point of departure.

INTRODUCTION

Most of the tanks disabled at the point of departure were tanks of Company "C" which was late in arriving owing to the delay on the railroad. Small repairs and regassing put seven in commission and they went with the Battalion Commander into action as a battle reserve....The going was extremely heavy owing to the difficult terrain which was made almost impassible by the five-day rain preceding the attack.

While crossing the TRENCH DES HOUBLONS (358.5-35.3) the tanks came under heavy shell fire and two tanks were put out of action by direct hits. One platoon of tanks with the infantry took the town of ESSEY (359.0-38.3) and again at the town of PANNES (358.6-39.0). The tanks rendered excellent service in reducing the resistance from the town and aiding the infantry to take many prisoners...

As the terrain was very difficult, breakdowns and ditching of the tanks were numerous. Lieutenant Saul not only gave his attention to his own duties, but directed the engineer officers who were present to make lanes for the tanks across the trenches and after selecting the routes and having the lanes made he personally led the tanks through the maze of the trenches and thus greatly expedited the advance of the tanks.

The battalion reserve owing to its fresh supply of gas and by taking full advantage of the tank lanes already made was able to pass to the town of PANNES where most of the tanks were obliged to stop for a refill of gas which had not yet arrived...

Tanks of the battalion had reached a point about 15 kilometers from the point of departure. They had been of material assistance to the infantry in capturing great quantities of machine guns, field pieces of large and small caliber and immense quantities of stores and supplies in the several towns.

The Boche located the infantry line and one tank which became disabled in a field to the south of BENEY and shelled these objectives intermittently through the night...

Then, almost two weeks later, on the first day of the Meuse-Argonne Offensive:

On the morning of the 26th, Colonel G. S. Patton, Jr., commanding the brigade of Tanks, was wounded while getting Tanks forward and rallying disorganized Infantrymen to attack enemy resistance.[10]

Patton requested Major Sereno E. Brett be placed in command of the brigade.[11] Major Brett in turn "placed Captain Compton in command of all tanks at the front, which included the 14th and 17th Groups French Tanks and the 344th and 345th Battalion Tank Corps."[12] Some of the "hardest" fighting of the war was still to come.

Of all the Meuse-Argonne fighting…between October 4 and 14 was the hardest which the American Army encountered in this war. The terrain was almost insurmountable. Between the Argonne forest and the Meuse river, a distance of 15 miles, the First American Army had in line on October 4, from the Meuse river west toward the forest: the 33rd Division (facing east along the river), 4th, 80th, 3rd, 32nd, 1st, 28th, and 77th Divisions (the latter within the forest).[13]

Many of Captain Compton's later entries—particularly those regarding combat and the problems he experienced working with tanks—were omitted from the brigade diary. Consider Compton's detailed report of September 12. Patton's brigade diary of the same day devotes two half sentences to the operations of Compton's 345th Battalion (… "345th Battalion operating with the 42nd Division…"

---

[10] Rockenbach, p. 51.

[11] Patton War Diary, September 26 entry.

[12] Patton War diary, September 27 entry.

[13] Shipley Thomas, The History of the A.E.F. (New York: George H. Doran Company, 1920), p. 291.

and "...345th Battalion rallied just south of town of BENEY...").

In part this could have been due to the limited space offered in the small preprinted booklets. In part it could be also have been due to the distance and preoccupation of the forward units during combat. In the pre-combat early days, the battalions might have had more time and personnel to run their diary entries to the brigade headquarters for purposes of informing the brigade diary. Once the action started, communications systems were in place to telegraph or telephone back to the brigade, but entries into the war diary would probably not have been a priority message.

> *The wireless outside corps headquarters was bringing news; the telegraph keys and the telephone were bringing more news over the wires; the aeroplanes were dropping message cylinders...You had more bits of information from officers who came in to report. One concerned the tanks, which had been having a characteristically merry time. A few had been stuck in crossing No Man's Land; a few always are.*[14]

There was perhaps time to get a quick burst of basic information into brigade headquarters for the diary entries by telephone or telegraph, but not much more. Compton's expansive entries on the days of combat, including some negative reporting on tank problems, might also not have been incorporated in their entirety due to Patton's personal stake in the success of tanks.

George S. Patton, Jr. was a West Point Graduate and career military officer. When he was first detailed to work with tanks in the fall of 1917, he was still a captain.[15] In quick succession he was promoted to major, lieutenant colonel and finally colonel in October 1918, less than a year

---

[14] Frederick Palmer, American in France (New York: Dodd, Mead and Company, 1918), p. 431.

[15] Blumenson, p. 435.

later.[16] He had commanded the American Tank Center in France and then the American Tank Brigade of the A.E.F.

A significant portion of Patton's personal prestige and career aspirations were tied to the success of this new battlefield invention. Sobering statistics such as those in Compton's September 12 diary entry listing the significant number of disabled tanks (nearly half of those engaging the enemy) were not as positive as perhaps Patton would have preferred.

While many books and scholarly articles have been written about Patton, only several paragraphs survive concerning C. H. (Claude Herod) Ranulf Compton's life.[17] He grew up in Indiana and attended Harvard University. He was a member of the New York National Guard before transferring to the U.S. Army Infantry and then deploying to France with the American Expeditionary Forces to be assigned to the newly organized Tank Corps.

Seven years older than Patton, Compton turned 40 the day after the Battle of St. Mihiel. While he had the same stake in the outcome of the war as Patton, he did not have the same stake in the future of tanks.

While Patton was reputed to be a strict disciplinarian, what come through from Compton's diary entries was his compassion for his men and understanding of their limits. Here is Compton's October 9 diary entry:

> It was impossible to get the tanks, such was their mechanical condition, to the front. Even when a single tank did arrive now and then it was manifestly unfit for battle. This added to the apprehension of the crews already near the end of their endurance. In spite of the conditions both officers and men continued to work on the tanks and tried with all their wits and strength to get them into battle, but without availing anything.

---

[16] Blumenson, p. 624.

[17] Biographical Dictionary of the United States Congress. http://bioguide.congress.gov/biosearch/biosearch1.asp

INTRODUCTION

Then again there was the matter of their personal relationship. After the American victory at St. Mihiel, the First Army was focused on their next operation in the Argonne.

> *Officers who had hoped for a little sleep once the Saint-Mihiel offensive was under way received "travel orders," with instructions to reach the Argonne area by hopping a motor-truck or in any way they could. Soldiers, after marching all night, might seek sleep in the villages if there were room in houses, barns, or haylofts. Blocks of traffic were frequent when some big gun or truck slewed into a slough in the darkness. The processions on these three roads from Saint-Mihiel represented only one of many movements from all directions of the Argonne sector. French units had to pass by our new front to that of the Fourth Army. A French officer at Bar-le-Duc, who had charge of routing all the traffic, was an old hand at this business of moving armies. He perfectly appreciated that curses were speeding toward his office from all four points of the compass where traffic was stalled or columns waited an interminably long time at cross-roads for their turn to move, or guns or tanks or anything else in all the varied assortment were not arriving on schedule time...[18]*

It was a mad rush to the next front, causing long delays in travel, including the trains carrying the tanks. But that did not stop Patton from venting his frustration at the late arrival of his men, especially Compton.

"*345th tanks not yet arrived...still madder with Capt. Compton. He is an ass*," Patton wrote from his location in Clermont, to his wife Beatrice back home on September 22.

In his personal diary for the same day, Patton wrote, "*Life is just one D___ thing after another. One whole battalion*

---

[18] Frederick Palmer, <u>Our Greatest Battle</u> (New York: Dodd, Mead & Company, 1919), pp. 26, 27.

has failed to show up and I can't find it. The battalion commander spent the day looking for a house instead of getting his tanks. He is a fool but I a greater one to trust him."[19]

In his diary for September 23 he wrote, "*Got all 345 tanks unloaded by daylight under shell fire but no casualties...Rained all day and a lot of shelling over us at Clermont. Cussed out Brett & Compton for carelessness, etc.*"[20]

However, in the official brigade war diary entries for the same dates, there are no negative remarks. What Patton had earlier perceived as failings on the part of Compton and his battalion were readily explained by the congestion of troops moving to the Argonne region, which caused delays in scheduled arrivals.

The following comment was written into the brigade war diary for September 22:

The 345th Battalion command post was moved to a point near the railroad station in Clermont, this move being necessary because the enemy had discovered and was shelling the old position. The new position was on the reverse slope of a hill and would afford good shelter for the men and tanks when they should arrive.

This was followed by the entry for September 23, which stated:

The 345th Battalion remained on trains enroute. As enemy shell fire had damaged part of the road bed, it was necessary to take a circuitous route to reach Clermont.

Both brigade entries closely matched Compton's battalion entries for the same dates.

---

[19] Blumenson, p. 606.
[20] Blumenson, p. 607.

INTRODUCTION

Compton's diary entries for September 22 and 23 explained his late arrival. Patton, by incorporating Compton's exculpatory entries for those days, accepted the reasons for the delay. Unfortunately, Patton's earlier negative assessments in his personal diary and letter home to Beatrice endure in some publications, disparaging Compton unfairly. This is regrettable, tainting as it does Compton's character and competence.

On October 12th, Captain Compton was relieved by Major Brett of the command of the forward tanks and returned to command the 345th Battalion. The battalion was removed from the front lines and withdrawn to the relative safety of the Tank Center at Bourg. Life became routine once again.

This is vividly reflected in Compton's last entries for October. As with the early entries in August, these were perfunctory references to schools and inspections. Borrowing a phrase, his combat experiences ended not with a bang, but a whimper.

The enemy forces were worn out and soon the war would be over. In his report on the Operations of the 304th at St. Mihiel, Patton complained that "Owing to the fact of the enemy's failure at serious resistance the full value of the Tanks was not susceptible of demonstration." He believed tanks had a future in warfare, but were denied the opportunity to fully showcase their capabilities. In that assessment, the German high command agreed.

The battle which had broken out on the Western Front at the end of September had meanwhile continued to rage...now we were weaker and one division failed after another. The number of shirkers behind the front increased alarmingly. The information posts, established to direct stragglers to their positions, were no longer equal to their task. The men who fought in the front line were heroes, but there were not enough of them for the long line. They felt themselves isolated. The men looked to their officers, who bore the brunt of the fighting. These officers, with their loyal men, achieved miracles of bravery...Our losses, however, were heavy. Our best men lay on the bloody battlefield...[21]

After the war, Samuel D. Rockenbach continued to advocate for the value of tanks in combat, serving two more years as the Chief of the Tank Corps before directing the Tank School at Ft. Meade, Maryland and finishing his army career as the commander of an artillery brigade. George S. Patton, Jr. and Sereno E. Brett (originally of the Oregon National Guard) also continued their active military careers; Patton destined for legendary status in yet another world war and Brett achieving the rank of Brigadier General before retiring.

For his actions in France, (then) Major Ranulf Compton earned the Purple Heart and the French Legion of Honor. He left the regular Army to return to the New York National Guard, where he served for several years as the Military Secretary to the governor. He continued to serve in other senior-level government positions in New York and Connecticut before being elected from Connecticut to serve one term in the U.S. House of Representatives. In his final years before retirement he owned and operated a broadcasting company.

It is because of Compton's diary that we are given a fuller, less vetted, picture of the first days of American tank warfare. We are also presented with a fuller picture of the man who irritated Patton but who, ironically, led his tanks into some of the toughest fighting of the war. Ranulf Compton had one heck of a story to tell. Through his own words in <u>War Diary 1918</u> he can finally tell it.

---

[21] General Ludendorff, <u>My War Memories 1914-1918</u>, Vol. II (London: Hutchinson & Co., 1919), pp. 739, 740.

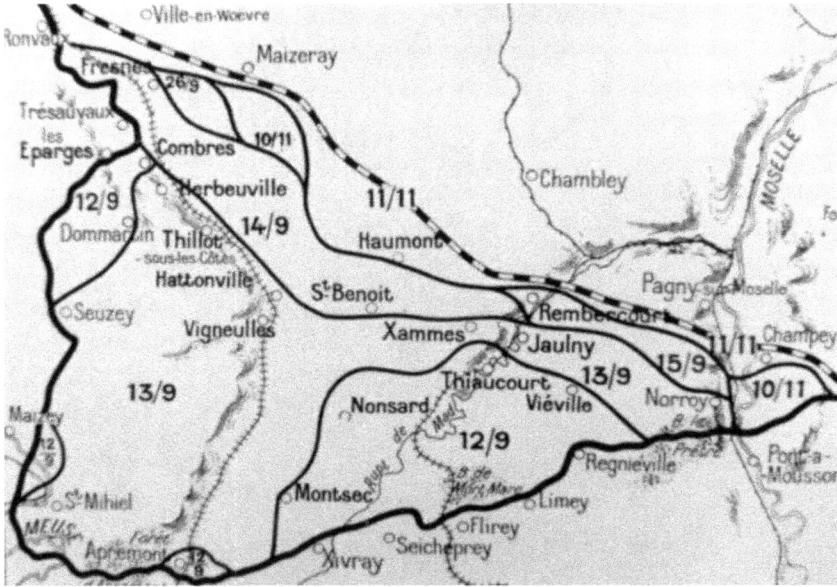

Showing the American-French Advance from
Sept. 12 (12/9) to
Nov. 11 (11/11), 1918.
<u>The Americans in the Great War</u>, Vol. II
(France: Michelin & Cie, Clermont-Ferrand, 1920), p. 18.

PATTON WAR DIARY - SEPTEMBER 1918

September 1918,
304th (1st) Brigade
Tank Corps.

This book is for one month;
do not tear out sheets.

WAR DIARY INSTRUCTIONS

1. Observe F. S. R., Paragraph 35.

2. This is the HISTORY of what your unit accomplishes, in other words, of OPERATIONS. Tell what actually happened; not what is supposed to have happened. Abstain from criticism.

3. Append all orders, messages, plans, sketches, etc.

4. Designate precisely each place and position occupied; assume that the reader never heard of any of them.

5. Note the personnel, losses and statistics of unit as changes occur; give dates, hours, state of weather, atmosphere and roads.

6. Enter the higher units to which you belong: brigades, divisions, corps, etc.

7. When maneuvering, always try to get the designations and positions of units next to you in line.

8. Tactical observations are particularly desired.

9. No erasures may be made in this Diary.

10. The C. O. must sign before the return is made at the end of the calendar month.

A. G. Printing Dept., G. H. Q. A. E. F., 1918.

Image of cover to Patton's War Diary for September 1918.

DATE: September 1, 1918
AVAILABLE FOR ALL DUTY: 48 Officers and 638 Men
WEATHER: Fair **ROADS:** Good

NARRATIVE OF OPERATIONS:[1]

Lieutenant Colonel George S. Patton Jr. (Brigade Commander) made arrangements at the 302nd Tank Center for the entrainment of the brigade. He left BOURG (302nd Tank Center) at 1:30 p.m. in company with Captain W. S. Etheridge (Brigade Supply Officer). A stop was made in CLERMONT and another at LIGNY-EN-BARROIS, the latter to arrange for detraining with G-4 First Army. Brigade Headquarters at BENOITE VAUX was reached at 12:30 a.m.

Captain Ranulf Compton (345th Battalion Commander) and Captains Gilfillan,[2] Williams,[3] and Barnard[4] (345th Company Commanders) arrived at Brigade Headquarters at 1:20 p.m. from BOURG and were taken to vicinity of HAUDIOMONT[5] (341.3-260.6) by the reconnaissance staff to study their sectors. They left Brigade Headquarters at 4:35 p.m. and returned to BOURG.

DATE: September 2, 1918
AVAILABLE FOR ALL DUTY: 49 Officers and 626 Men
WEATHER: Fair **ROADS:** Good

NARRATIVE OF OPERATIONS:

Brigade Headquarters moved to larger accommodations but still remaining in BENOITE VAUX with Headquarters, 5th

---

[1] Editor's Note: Diary entries September 1 through 9 are italicized to indicate they were handwritten by Patton personally. Beginning September 10 diary entries were written by someone other than Patton, although Patton continued to sign each day's entry and at times wrote in corrections or additional comments. Beginning with the September 10 diary entry, all subsequent comments in Patton's handwriting are italicized AND bolded for easier reference.

[2] Captain Dean M. Gilfillan.

[3] Captain William H. Williams.

[4] Captain Courtney H. Barnard.

[5] Spelled Haudimont by Captain Compton in battalion September 1 entry.

Army Corps. Sectors of Divisions of 5th Army Corps changed and brigade plans had to be changed (see map attached to August War Diary).[6]

The enemy area was observed by the reconnaissance staff all day. All preliminary reconnaissance and plans for the attack were completed on this date.

The two battalions of the brigade moved out of their billets and went into camp in shelter tents near the station of BRENNES (302nd Tank Center) where all tanks, transportation and equipment was concentrated.

```
                HEADQUARTERS FIRST ARMY.
        OFFICE OF THE CHIEF OF TANK CORPS.
                                   3 September, 1918.
From:     Commanding General, 1st Army.
To:       Commanding General, 4th and 5th Corps.
          Commanding Officer, 1st T.C. Brigade.
Subject: Attachment of the 1st Brigade, T.C.
        1. Pursuant to instructions of the Commanding
General 1st Army the 1st American T.C. Brigade is
relieved from duty with the 5th Corps and attached
to the 4th Corps. The Brigade Commander and his
staff will proceed immediately and report to the
Commanding General 4th Corps for temporary duty.
                   By direction:
               S. D. Rockenbach,
           Brigadier General, U.S.A.
               Chief of Tank Corps.
```

DATE: September 3, 1918
ORGANIZATION: Brigade Headquarters
FROM: Benoite Vaux **HOUR:** 5:15 p.m. **TO:** Ecrouves
HOUR: 2:00 a.m.
AVAILABLE FOR ALL DUTY: 48 Officers and 640 Men
WEATHER: Warm **ROADS:** Good

---

[6] Not found with archived diary collection.

3

NARRATIVE OF OPERATIONS:

The Brigade Commander and the reconnaissance staff went to observation posts to study the enemy area and in addition to select a battle command post.

First Lieutenant Bolan[7] (345th Battalion Reconnaissance Officer) delivered a message to return to 5th Army Corps Headquarters immediately. This message was received at point 39.7-57.8 at 4:30 p.m. The 1st (Provisional) Tank Brigade was relieved from the 5th Army Corps and attached to the 4th Army Corps for duty.

Brigade Headquarters packed up and moved to ECROUVES via LIGNY-EN-BARROIS, the first echelon at 6:30 p.m. Headquarters were in the same building occupied by the 3rd Tank Brigade (Colonel Pullen[8] Commanding). The second echelon of Brigade Headquarters arrived at 2:00 a.m.

DATE: September 4, 1918
AVAILABLE FOR ALL DUTY: 47 Officers and 647 Men
WEATHER: Fair **ROADS:** Fair

NARRATIVE OF OPERATIONS:

The Brigade Commander and the reconnaissance staff reconnoitered the area of the 4th Army Corps selecting tentative stages of advance and carefully studying the enemy area from in front of BEAUMONT.

HEADQUARTERS FIRST ARMY.
AMERICAN EXPEDITIONARY FORCES, FRANCE.
5th September, 1918
SPECIAL ORDERS)
    No. 135)
            C O R R E C T E D C O P Y.
    1. The following allotment of Tank Corps troops is announced:
    1st American Brigade (2 bns.) and 2 groups French, to the FOURTH CORPS, detraining point ANSAUVILLE.

---

[7] First Lieutenant Harry W. Bolan, Tank Corps.
[8] Lieutenant Colonel D. D. Pullen, Tank Corps (CE).

505th French Regiment (3 bns.) and one French groupement, to the FIRST CORPS, detraining point BOIS VILLERS-en-HAYE and BOIS de la RAPPE.

2. The Commanding Officer of the FIRST AMERICAN BRIGADE will report to the Commanding General, FOURTH CORPS, for temporary. The Chief of Staff, Tank Corps, 1st Army, will report to the Commanding General, FIRST CORPS, to carry out his special instructions in connection with movements of the Tank Corps Troops assigned to that Corps.

BY COMMAND OF GENERAL PERSHING:
H. A. DRUM,
Chief of Staff.

————————

DATE: September 5, 1918
AVAILABLE FOR ALL DUTY: 47 Officers and 645 Men
WEATHER: Fair **ROADS:** Good
NARRATIVE OF OPERATIONS:

Leaving Brigade Headquarters at 6:30 a.m. The Brigade Commander and the Brigade Reconnaissance Officer went to the front, studied the enemy area and reconnoitered for positions of departure and means of crossing the RUPT DE MAD RIVER. This stream was followed out to the bridge at XIVRAY-ET-MARVOISIN. The enemy terrain was later studied from the Regimental Observation Post in BEAUMONT and Observation Post Joseph in BOIS DU JURY.

Returning to Brigade Headquarters at 3:40 p.m. the plan for the use of tanks was written and submitted to the Chief of Staff, 4th Army Corps.

DATE: September 6, 1918
AVAILABLE FOR ALL DUTY: 47 Officers and 643 Men
WEATHER: Rainy **ROADS:** Fair
NARRATIVE OF OPERATIONS:

Major Sereno E. Brett (344th Battalion Commander) and Captains Weed,[9] Semmes[10] and English[11] arrived at Brigade Headquarters at 11:25 a.m. and were taken to the front and

---

[9] Captain Newell P. Weed.
[10] Captain Harry Hodges Semmes.
[11] Captain Math L. English.

shown their sectors. The enemy organization, obstacles of terrain and landmarks were carefully impressed upon them by the reconnaissance officers.

The sector of the 1st (Provisional) Brigade Tank Corps was also that of the 42nd and 1st Divisions. The Brigade Commander visited the Chief of Staff, 42nd and 1st Divisions and coordinated the tanks and other arms.

Major Chanoine,[12] Commandant French Groups of Tanks, reported at 1:15 p.m.

Maps and photos (vertical and oblique) were requested from G-2, 4th Army Corps for the Brigade.

Brigadier General Rockenbach, Chief of Tank Corps A.E.F., called and inspected Brigade Headquarters.

DATE: September 7, 1918
AVAILABLE FOR ALL DUTY: 47 Officers and 638 Men
WEATHER: Cloudy **ROADS:** Fair

NARRATIVE OF OPERATIONS:

Detraining points and all stages of the advance were selected and routes to and from these points of rest were carefully reconnoitered.

MENIL-LA-TOUR was selected for the Repair and Salvage Company (321st Company) and the main supply dump for the brigade.

Routes and stages of the advance were reconnoitered for the French Groups of Tanks. The Brigade Commander went over the entire plan with Major Chanoine.

Captain Compton went to BERNECOURT and established 345th Battalion Command Post. Company A, 345th Battalion and one-half Company B, 345th Battalion detrained at BRENNES to move to BOIS DE LA HAZELLE (359.8-31.7) near BERNECOURT.

The 14th and 17th Groups of French Tanks arrived at BOIS DE LA REINE during the night, were detrained and camouflaged before daylight.

---

[12] Chefs d'Escadrons Chanoine C.M.M.

DATE: September 8, 1918
AVAILABLE FOR ALL DUTY: 47 Officers and 648 Men
WEATHER: Raining **ROADS:** Fair

NARRATIVE OF OPERATIONS:

Company A, 344th Battalion and one-half Company B, 344th Battalion entrained and left BRENNES at 4:00 p.m.

Arrangements were made to get the French Groups of Tanks up to the position of readiness in BOIS DE LA HAZELLE (359.8-31.7) and these tanks moved up during the night.

DATE: September 9, 1918
ORGANIZATION: 344th Battalion **FROM:** Brennes
HOUR: 5:00 a.m. **TO:** Boucq Station **HOUR:** 6 p.m.
DISTANCE: 150 kilometers
AVAILABLE FOR ALL DUTY: 47 Officers and 648 Men
WEATHER: Raining **ROADS:** Poor

NARRATIVE OF OPERATIONS:

The first section of the 344th Battalion (Company A and one-half Company B) started to detrain at BOUCQ STATION at noon. The tanks were placed in woods nearby until dusk when they proceeded to the position of readiness at FAUX BOIS DE NAUGINSARD point 355.2-226.1 map Montsec 1/50,000, a distance of 9 kilometers.

The second section of 344th Battalion (one-half Company B and Company C) left BRENNES (302 Tank Center) at 5:00 a.m. arriving at BOUCQ STATION at 6:00 p.m. and detraining started at once. At dusk this section started to move to the position of readiness in FAUX BOIS DE NAUGINSARD.

Sixteen tanks were segregated from the 344th Battalion for the brigade reserve.

DATE: September 10, 1918
ORGANIZATION: 345th Battalion **FROM:** Brennes
TO: Bois de Rehanne **HOUR:** 8 p.m.
ORGANIZATION: 344th Battalion **FROM:** Brennes
HOUR: 5:00 a.m. **TO:** Faux Bois de Nauginsard
HOUR: 9:00 a.m. **DISTANCE:** 9 kilometers
AVAILABLE FOR ALL DUTY: 47 Officers and 648 Men
WEATHER: Raining **ROADS:** Poor **HEALTH:** Good
CAMP: Fair

[Notes at left margin of diary page:
"Map. Mort Mare 1/20000, St. Mihiel-C. 1/20000, and
Montsec 1/50000."]

NARRATIVE OF OPERATIONS:

The first section 345th Battalion (Company A and one-half Company B) detrained at point 362.5-28.5 north of BOIS DE REHANNE at 8 p.m. All tanks were camouflaged in BOIS DE LA HAZELLE point 359.8-31.7 by 3:00 a.m.[13]

The second section 344th Battalion reached lying-in position FAUX BOIS DE NAUGINSARD point 255.2-226.1 and 344th Battalion Headquarters established. Work of equipping, getting necessary gas and oil and making repairs progressing rapidly in both battalions.

Field Order #1 1st Provisional Brigade published this date. This is the first order directing an attack of American tanks ever published. (Copy attached.)[14]

DATE: September 11, 1918
ORGANIZATION: 344th Battalion
FROM: Faux Bois de Nauginsard **HOUR:** 9 p.m.
AVAILABLE FOR ALL DUTY: 47 Officers and 648 Men
WEATHER: Rain **ROADS:** Poor **HEALTH:** Good
CAMP: Fair

[Notes at left margin of diary page:
"Maps: Mort Mare 1/20000, St. Mihiel 1/20000."]

---

[13] At this point, Patton delegated the task of recording the daily diary entries. However, as evidenced by the original war diaries, he continued to review and personally sign each day for all the months transcribed here. Any additional comments written in Patton's own hand will be italicized and bolded for easy reference.

[14] Copy not found with diary collection.

8

NARRATIVE OF OPERATIONS:

The 345th Battalion still waiting for the second section of their tank train. Battalion remained in camp at lying-in position BOIS DE LA HAZELLE point 359.8-31.7 making preparations for the attack.

The 344th remained in camp at lying-in position FAUX BOIS DE NAUGINSARD point 355.2-226.1 continuing preparations for the attack.

Reconnaissance officers both battalions continue reconnoitering the front. Battalion Field Order and Orders published this date. (Copy attached.)[15]

```
        GENERAL HEADQUARTERS, TANK CORPS
        American Expeditionary Forces.
                            September 12, 1918.
General Orders
No. 16.
        1. In compliance with instructions from the
Adjutant General of the Army, the designations of
the following units organized in France are changed
as indicated:
        311 Center, T.C.      to 302 Center, T.C.
        316 Company T.C.      to 321 Company, T.C.
        326 Battalion, T.C.  to 344 Battalion, T.C.
        327 Battalion, T.C.  to 345 Battalion, T.C.
        By command of Brigadier General Rockenbach
                GEORGE J. CROSBY
                Captain, Tank Corps,
                    Adjutant.
```

---

[15] Copy not found with archived diary collection.

DATE: September 12, 1918
ORGANIZATION: 344th Battalion **TO:** Nonsard
DISTANCE: 12 Kilometers
ORGANIZATION: 345th Battalion **FROM:** Jump of line
HOUR: 5:00 a.m. **TO:** Bois Beney **DISTANCE:** 15 kilometers
AVAILABLE FOR ALL DUTY: 47 Officers and 645 Men
WEATHER: Rainy **ROADS:** Poor **HEALTH:** Good
CAMP: Fair **LOSSES:** 2 Officers wounded; 3 Men killed
CAPTURES: 80 Men, 10 Guns

NARRATIVE OF OPERATIONS:

General Order #16 General Headquarters Tank Corps this date changing designations of 326th and 327th Battalions to 344th and 345th Battalions respectively (copy attached).

This was "D" Day, "H" Hour at 5:00 a.m. Brigade supported the 4th Army Corps (1st Army), 344th Battalion operating with 1st Division; 345th Battalion operating with the 42nd Division. Two companies of each battalion went into the attack with two platoons in the front line and one platoon in support. The third company of each battalion ~~combined to form the brigade reserve under command of First Lieutenant H. E. Gibbs~~[16] *were in battalion reserve. Thirty reserve and training tanks were placed in sector 344th Battalion as brigade reserve under Lieutenant Gibbs.*

The day's objectives were in every case attained, despite the bad muddy conditions. The brigade reserve joined the 344th Battalion on the TRENCH MOULON position and took an active part in the advance from then on. At the end of day's fighting 344th Battalion and battalion reserve rallied just south of NONSARD; 345th Battalion rallied just south of town of BENEY. (Correction made from GSP)

---

[16] First Lieutenant Harry E. Gibbs, Tank Corps.

DATE: September 13, 1918
ORGANIZATION: 344th Battalion **FROM:** Nonsard
HOUR: 3:00 p.m. **TO:** Vigneulles **HOUR:** 12:00 m.n.
ORGANIZATION: 345th Battalion **FROM:** Beney
TO: Bois de Beney 358.1-243.0
AVAILABLE FOR ALL DUTY: 46 Officers and 643 Men
WEATHER: Rain a.m. Clear p.m. **ROADS:** Poor
HEALTH: Good **CAMP:** Fair **LOSSES:** [1 or 0 - digit unclear]
Officers wounded; 3 Men wounded

NARRATIVE OF OPERATIONS:

Due to bad road conditions, no supplies arrived during the night. By draining all the tanks, the 344th Battalion was able to supply seven of their tanks which moved forward to VIGNEULLES and thence to HATTON CHATTEL.[17] Supplies arrived at 3:00 p.m. and the remaining tanks moved forward to VIGNEULLES.

At 5:00 a.m. 345th Battalion with 15 tanks reported to Brigadier General MacArthur and were instructed by him to lay in readiness at BOIS DE BENEY and await orders. Per V.O.C.O.[18] the battalion moved from BOIS DE BENEY to BOIS DE THIAUCOURT at 8:00 p.m. At 11:55 p.m. orders were received from Lieutenant Colonel Patton "to go to assistance of infantry against enemy counterattack." The tanks were made ready but the attack did not take place.

HEADQUARTERS FOURTH ARMY CORPS
G-3

September 14, 1918.
M E S S A G E
To: Commanding General, 1st Division.
       Commanding General, 42nd Division.
       Commanding Officer, 1st Tank Brigade.
       1. The 1st and 2nd Battalions, 1st Tank Brigade, and detachment of 18 French medium tanks are detached from the 1st and 42nd Divisions and will assemble tonight in the southern edge of BOIS THIAUCOURT under command of the Commanding Officer, 1st Tank Brigade.

---

[17] Fr. Hattonchâtel.

[18] Verbal orders of the commanding officer.

2. All tanks will move on the night of September 15/16 to the southern edge BOIS QUART DE RESERVE.

3. All tanks will move on the night of September 16/17 to the northern edge of FORET DE LA REINE. Movement will only be made during hours of darkness and every care will be taken to avoid hostile aerial observation. Tanks will use only unimproved roads or tracks or will move across country.

4. Officers will be sent in advance to reconnoiter routes and bivouacs.

5. Railhead unchanged.

6. Change of P.C.[19] will be promptly reported.

By command of Major General Dickman

Stuart Heintzelman,
Chief of Staff.

———————

DATE: September 14, 1918
ORGANIZATION: 344th Battalion **FROM:** Vigneulles
HOUR: 7:30 a.m. **TO:** Woel **HOUR:** 11:30 p.m.
ORGANIZATION: 345th Battalion [sic]
AVAILABLE FOR ALL DUTY: 46 Officers and 643 Men
WEATHER: Rain **ROADS:** Poor **HEALTH:** Good
CAMP: Fair **LOSSES:** 2 Officers wounded; 2 Men wounded
CAPTURES: 2 Men

NARRATIVE OF OPERATIONS:

Liaison with 1st Division having been broken and no information as to their position or intentions received, it was decided to move forward.

The 344th Battalion moved forward to ST. MAURICE where word was received that American outposts were holding line of hills behind ST. MAURICE–HATTON CHATTEL–VIGNEULLES. As there were no signs of the enemy, the battalion again moved forward and finally camped at 11:30 a.m. in the vicinity of WOEL.

From this position, two patrols of tanks were sent out to gain contact with the enemy, which they did at JONVILLE, returning with all tanks at 5:00 p.m.

---

[19] Post of Command or Command Post.

At 6:00 p.m. battalion moved ½ kilometer south to avoid artillery fire. At 9:05 p.m. message received from Commanding Officer, 1st Brigade Tank Corps, to proceed to THIAUCOURT, a distance of 12 kilometers.

March commenced at 9:20 p.m. and battalion arrived at 5:00 a.m. September 15 at point 357-251; map MONTSEC 1:50,000.

345th Battalion spent the day making minor repairs at BOIS DE THIAUCOURT. Upon receipt of orders from Headquarters, 1st Brigade Tank Corps, 345th Battalion moved out at 7:00 p.m. and proceeded to BOIS DE LA HAZELLE arriving at 1:00 a.m. September 15th.

The patrols encounter between WOEL and JONVILLE was creditable to the light tanks engaged. These tanks under Lieutenant McCluer[20] attacked one battalion of German infantry light machine guns and 4-77 guns and drove them 6 kilometers capturing the guns and entering the town of JONVILLE on the Hindenburg Line. Lieutenant McCluer was wounded while trying to attack a 77 gun to the back of his tank to bring it out of action. This was a [word indecipherable], tank action as no infantry was within 8 kilometers.

DATE: September 15, 1918
AVAILABLE FOR ALL DUTY: 47 Officers and 666 Men
WEATHER: Fair **ROADS:** Fair **HEALTH:** Good **CAMP:** Fair
NARRATIVE OF OPERATIONS:

The 344th Battalion spent the day at BOIS DE THIAUCOURT, resting and making minor repairs. At 7:30 p.m., per V.O.C.O. Battalion Commander, battalion commenced 12 kilometer march to BOIS DE LA HAZELLE. The tanks arrived during the night and battalion went into camp at north edge of BOIS DE LA HAZELLE, on the morning of September 16th.

The 345th Battalion moved to BERNECOURT, where companies where reorganized and disabled tanks brought in by the help of 100 German prisoners. It was

---

[20] Second Lieutenant Edward McCluer.

13

found that by using a long rope 100 men could pull a tank out of a hole.

HEADQUARTERS - TANK CORPS - 1st ARMY.
Special Orders)   16 September, 1918.
No. 2   )
    1. Commanding Officers of the 1st and 3rd Tank Brigades, having reported will proceed in liaison with Colonel Wahl[21] to RAMPONT and establish temporary headquarters there and then proceed to carry out special verbal instructions given them by the Chief of Tank Corps.
    By command of Brigadier General Rockenbach,
                W. MILLER,
          1st Lieut. Tank Corps,
            Adjutant.

HEADQUARTERS   FIRST ARMY
American Expeditionary Forces France.
    G-3   16 September, 1918.
SPECIAL ORDERS)
   No. 211   )
    1. Headquarters, 1st Tank Brigade is relieved from duty with the 4th Corps, and will proceed at once to report to the Chief of Tank Corps, 1st Army and carry out his instructions.
    2. Headquarters, 3rd Tank Brigade is relieved from duty with the First Corps and will proceed at once to report to the Chief of Tank Corps, 1st Army to carry out his instructions.
    By Command of General Pershing:
           H. A. Drum
           Chief of Staff

---

[21] Colonel Wahl, Commander of the French 1st Assault Artillery Brigade attached to A.E.F. Tank Corps.

DATE: September 16, 1918
AVAILABLE FOR ALL DUTY: 45 Officers and 632 Men
WEATHER: Fair **ROADS:** Fair **HEALTH:** Good **CAMP:** Fair
NARRATIVE OF OPERATIONS:

344th Battalion spent the day at BOIS DE LA HAZELLE repairing and resupplying tanks. Belated tanks coming into camp throughout the day.

The 345th Battalion spent the day in camp at BERNECOURT reorganizing and repairing tanks.

Copy of President Wilson's message to General Pershing commending the achievements of the Army at ST. MIHIEL received.

Copy of letter of commendation from Commanding General, 1st Division received.

Copy of both letters attached.

```
September 15, 1918.
Commanding General, 1st Corps.
Commanding General, 4th Corps.
Commanding General, 5th Corps.
Commanding General, 3rd Corps.
Commanding General, 11 Colonial Corps, (French).
Number 105, Sec. G.S. PERIOD The Army Commander
directs that the following messages from the
President of the United States be transmitted to you
for transmission to all troops of your command Quote
Washington, September 14th PERIOD To General John J.
Pershing, American Expeditionary Forces, France
PERIOD Accept my warmest congratulations on the
brilliant achievements of the Army under your
command PERIOD The boys have done what was expected
of them and their Chief PERIOD Please convey to all
concerned my grateful and affectionate thanks PERIOD
Signed Woodrow Wilson PERIOD Quote
                    DRUM
```

Headquarters First Division
American Expeditionary Forces,
France, September 15, 1918.
From: Commanding General, First Division
To: Commanding Officer, 1st Tank Brigade, Amer. E.F.
Subj: Conduct of the 326th Battalion of Tanks during
operations against St. Mihiel Salient.

    1. I desire to express formally, and in
writing, my thanks for the splendid and wholly
satisfactory work of the 326th Tank Battalion,
attached to this Division during the recent
operations against the St. Mihiel Salient.

    2. The operations of the tanks in the most
difficult country and under the most trying
conditions of weather, mud and swollen streams, were
carried out with the same vigor, skill and devotion
in which they were conceived. In this connection, I
particularly desire to commend by name their
Commander, Major Brett, Tank Corps.

    3. The command feels that the tanks have saved
many American Lives and greatly contribute to this
noteworthy success of American arms. I express the
thanks of the command to you and to Major Brett and
to his splendid Battalion.

C. P. SUMMERALL,
Major General, U.S.A.

DATE: September 17, 1918
AVAILABLE FOR ALL DUTY: 45 Officers and 631 Men
WEATHER: Rain **ROADS:** Fair **HEALTH:** Good **CAMP:** Fair
NARRATIVE OF OPERATIONS:

The 344th Battalion remained in Camp at BOIS DE LA HAZELLE, repairing tanks. Battalion Reconnaissance Officer established entraining points.

The 345th Battalion remained in camp at BERNECOURT reorganizing and repairing tanks.

HEADQUARTERS FIRST ARMY
AMERICAN EXPEDITIONARY FORCES, FRANCE
G-3

18 Sept. 1918.

SPECIAL ORDERS)   SECRET
NO. 243)

1. The following allotment of Tank Corps troops is announced:

> (a) 1st American Brigade (2 Bns.) and group French SCHNEIDER to the FIRST CORPS — detraining point RECICOURT.
>
> (b) 505th Regiment (3 Bns.) and French two groups ST. CHAMOND to the FIFTH CORPS — detraining point DOMBASLE.
>
> (c) The 504th Regiment (less 1 Battalion) and group ST. CHAMOND (12 Tanks) to the Fifth Corps — detraining point DOMBASLE.
>
> (d) The Commanding Officer and Headquarters, 3d Brigade to the FIFTH CORPS, for liaison with the Corps and the French units attached thereto.

By command of General PERSHING:
H.A. DRUM
Chief of Staff

DATE: September 18, 1918
AVAILABLE FOR ALL DUTY: 45 Officers and 625 Men
WEATHER: Rain **ROADS:** Fair **HEALTH:** Good **CAMP:** Fair
NARRATIVE OF OPERATIONS:

The 344th Battalion remained in camp at BOIS DE LA HAZELLE, repair and supply work continuing.

The 345th Battalion submitted to Chief of Tank Corps a report of operations and a report on status of personnel of the battalion. Pursuant to orders from Commanding Officer, 302nd Centre, Tank Corps, 10 tanks were placed on detached service and loaded on automobile trucks. They were held until following day. ***Lieutenant Higgins[22] (nominated Captain) was in charge of these tanks under orders of Maj. J. W. Viner.***

---

[22] First Lieutenant Ernest A. Higgins.

17

DATE: September 19, 1918
AVAILABLE FOR ALL DUTY: 45 Officers and 625 Men
WEATHER: Rain **ROADS:** Fair **HEALTH:** Good
CAMP: Good

NARRATIVE OF OPERATIONS:

The 344th Battalion still encamped at BOIS DE LA HAZELLE. At 4:00 p.m. five tanks under command Lieutenant Gibbs left to report to Lieutenant Higgins at BERNECOURT. At 8:00 p.m. 13 trucks and part of personnel left for CLERMONT-EN-ARGONNE traveling all night. Tanks were loaded on train at BERNECOURT.

The 10 tanks of the 345th Battalion loaded the previous day on trucks were reloaded on flat cars on the DECAUVILLE RAILROAD and proceeded as per instructions. Remainder of battalion personnel on light duty and finished repair work on tanks. Captain Compton reported to Headquarters, 4th Corps and received road orders for movement into another sector.

Received the following Letters of Commendation –
1) From C.G., A.E.F. to Chief of Tank Corps.
2) From Chief of Tank Corps to Lieutenant Colonel G.S. Patton, Jr.

Copies attached.

```
            HEADQUARTERS - TANK CORPS - 1st ARMY.
                                 18 September 1918.
Lieut-Colonel G.S. Patton, Jr.
Commanding 1st Brigade American Tank Corps.
My dear Colonel Patton:
        Attached is a copy of a letter received this
date from the Commander-in-Chief, which I wish you
to convey to the officers and men of your command,
who were engaged with you in the recent offensive
against the St. Mihiel Salient.
        In addition to this, express to them my
appreciation of the hard, laborious and excellent
work which was done by your brigade prior to the
engagement and then to the dash and vim of their
attack in which you were so ably assisted by the IV
Group Schneider, French. Preceding our infantry you
```

not only saved them many losses but by planting your red, yellow and blue flag well in advance and on the Hindenburg line you had a very great, far reaching and disastrous effect on the enemy.

Your brigade, has in their baptism of fire, established a record that the corps, will by its best endeavors, attempt to perpetuate. Don't forget in this that the men who were slaving to get your supplies up and maintain your communications are equally worthy of praise and that their work was done without the stimulant of combat.

I most heartily thank you and your men and my enthusiasm for you all is sobered only by the thought of the sorrow of the families of the men who were killed. To those families of men who were killed I want the Company Commanders to write fully, so that they may know of the sons and brother who as valorously, as the Knight of Old, charged the enemy. Their graves well within the enemy's lines are monuments to be proud of.

Very sincerely yours,

S.D. Rockenbach

Brigadier General, U.S.A.

Chief of Tank Corps

AMERICAN EXPEDITIONARY FORCES,

OFFICE OF THE COMMANDER - in - CHIEF

France, September 16, 1918.

Brigadier General S.D. Rockenbach,

Chief of Tank Corps,

First Army, A.E.F.

France.

My dear General:

Please accept my sincere congratulations on the successful and important part taken by the officers and men of the Tank Corps in the first offensive of the First American Army on September 12th and 13th. The courageous dash and vigor of our troops has thrilled our countrymen and evoked the enthusiasm of our allies. Please convey to your command my heartfelt appreciation of their splendid work. I am proud of you all.

Sincerely yours,

JOHN J. PERSHING.

19

DATE: September 20, 1918
AVAILABLE FOR ALL DUTY: 46 Officers and 632 Men
WEATHER: Cloudy **ROADS:** Fair **HEALTH:** Good
CAMP: Fair

NARRATIVE OF OPERATIONS:

The 344th Battalion trucks enroute for CLERMONT-EN-ARGONNE arrived at 4:00 p.m. and waited along road just outside CLERMONT until night, when they moved into woods 2 kilometers north of CLERMONT at point 05-61.2, map ARGONNE-MONTFAUCON. At 1:00 a.m. the first section left BERNECOURT. At 9:00 a.m. the second section left BERNECOURT. Both sections arrived during the night and proceeded to woods where trucks were located.

The 345th Battalion left their camp at 1:00 p.m. and proceeded to the entraining point 362.8-28.4, 2 kilometers south of BERNECOURT, arriving at 4:00 p.m. The men and tanks waited here during the night for rail transportation.

DATE: September 21, 1918
AVAILABLE FOR ALL DUTY: 48 Officers and 623 Men
WEATHER: Rain **ROADS:** Fair **HEALTH:** Good
CAMP: Good

NARRATIVE OF OPERATIONS:

The 344th lay in at woods all day, but as they were under direct enemy observation from VAUQUOIS HILL, Major Brett ordered them to move to HAUTE-PRISE FARM, 2 kilometers further north and nearer the enemy but a concealed position. The battalion moved accordingly at 6:00 p.m. The enemy's artillery was active, firing in the back area.

The 345th Battalion first section left entraining point at noon; the second section left at 6:00 p.m. The Battalion Command Post was moved by truck and automobile to a woods about ~~one~~ ½ *GSP* kilometer north of CLERMONT-EN-ARGONNE.

20

DATE: September 22, 1918
AVAILABLE FOR ALL DUTY: 50 Officers and 636 Men
WEATHER: Cloudy **ROADS:** Fair **HEALTH:** Good
CAMP: Good

NARRATIVE OF OPERATIONS:

The 344th Battalion remained in camp at HAUTE-PRISE FARM resting men and preparing for expected offensive. Tanks used to pull trucks into camp. Our camp vacated last evening was heavily shelled by the enemy today.

The 345th Battalion Command Post was moved to a point near the railroad station in CLERMONT, this move being necessary because the enemy had discovered and was shelling the old position. The new position was on the reverse slope of a hill and would afford good shelter for the men and tanks when they should arrive.

DATE: September 23, 1918
AVAILABLE FOR ALL DUTY: 45 Officers and 611 Men
WEATHER: Rain **ROADS:** Poor **HEALTH:** Good
CAMP: Good

NARRATIVE OF OPERATIONS:

The 344th Battalion established forward dumps of gas and oil by night at ABANCOURT FARM and northwest of COTES DE FORIMONT. A complete reconnaissance was made of positions between eastern edge of FORET D'ARGONNE and STREAM BUANTHE. The Battalion Commander in conference with the Chiefs of Staff, 28th and 35th Divisions.

The 345th Battalion remained on trains enroute. As enemy shell fire had damaged part of the road bed, it was necessary to take a circuitous route to reach CLERMONT.

DATE: September 24, 1918
AVAILABLE FOR ALL DUTY: 45 Officers and 611 Men
WEATHER: Rain **ROADS:** Poor **HEALTH:** Good
CAMP: Good

NARRATIVE OF OPERATIONS:

The 344th Battalion remained in camp. Field Order #2 1st Brigade Tank Corps received (copy attached).[23] 1st Brigade Tank Corps to assist attack of 1st Army Corps. Dispositions shown with attached order.

The 345th Battalion with 56 tanks plus 3 tanks belonging to the 344th Battalion arrived, unloaded and went into camp on the reverse side of hill, in woods, near detraining point CLERMONT, before 10:00 a.m.

```
          HEADQUARTERS 344 BATTALION, TANK CORPS
                 FRANCE, 25 Sept. 1918
Field Order)
    No. 2.  )
Maps: MEZIERES
    BAR-LE-DUC         1/80000
    VERDUN A
    FORET D'ARGONNE    1/20000
1. (a) The First Corps (American) is to attack D day
at H hour between the limits shown on map previously
furnished.
    (b) Order of Battle (right to left)
         35th Div.   28th Div.   77th Div.
2. This Battalion will support the advance of the
35th and 28th Divisions.
3. Detailed Instructions.
    (a) Companies "A" and "C," operating with the
35th Division will leave from No. 2 position at such
time that the leading company (Company "C") will be
at its point of departure immediately behind the
infantry in time to advance at H hour ahead of the
infantry.
    (b) Company "C" will support the entire front of
the 35th Division between the AIRE RIVER and the
BUANTHE STREAM.
    (c) Company "A" will follow Company "C" at a
distance of approximately 500 M., avoiding becoming
engaged, cross the BUANTHE STREAM near CHEPPY and
support that portion of the 35th Division operating
on the east side of the BUANTHE STREAM.
```

---

[23] Not found with archived diary collection.

(d) Company "B" will support the advance of the 28th Division between the limits shown on map previously furnished. It will leave its No. 2 position near the FARM ABANCOURT at such time to move forward ahead of the infantry at H hour.

(e) On reaching the Corps objective Company Commanders of "A" and "C" Companies will report the number of tanks still available for further progress to the Battalion Commander at BAULNY by runner, and will include in this report the average amount of gasoline per tank. On reaching the Corps objective (see map furnished) the C.O. "B" Company will check the number of tanks and quantity of gasoline available, and, if needed, will call on the company of the 345th Battalion supporting him to take up the advance.

(f) On reaching the American Army Objective (see map furnished) the Company Commanders will assemble their companies as follows:

For "A" and "C" Companies - at point 224 North edge of MONT TRABEAU[24]

For "B" Company at point 1169 at ravine West of BAULNY.

At these points companies will refill with gas and oil and arrange to follow in support to the lines.

COMBINED ARMY 1ST PHASE AND
COMBINED ARMY 1ST OBJECTIVE

It is to be distinctly understood that the companies of the 344th Battalion will be relieved by the companies of the 345th Battalion on reaching the American Army objective and that from this point on the 344th Battalion will be in support until needed.

(g) All tank crews, runners and reserve crews will enter the fight with canteen full of water and 2½ days reserve rations in tanks or on their persons. Men will wear blouses and carry one blanket.

4. Supply.

(a) The Battalion Rear Officer will arrange to detail one-third of his command to each company, to follow at a distance of 2000 to 3000 M.

(b) The Battalion Medical Officer will detail one sergeant and two privates to accompany Company "B" and will arrange to follow "A" and "C" Companies

---

[24] Montrebeau.

with the remainder of his detachment at a distance
of 2000 to 3000 M.

(c) <u>GAS AND OIL</u> - Each Company Commander before
leaving present location will arrange to carry
sufficient gas and oil on tanks to refill at No. 2
position. At No. 2 position Company Commanders will
see that two (2) small bedons (now at No. 2
position), in the correct proportion of oil, heavy
oil and gas for each platoon, will be tied on the
tail of each tank and carried into action. Before
leaving present location all reserve tanks will be
pooled and redistributed to companies. These tanks
will carry at least six (6) small bedons each, using
the gunners compartment. One Officer from each
company will be detailed by the Company Commanders
to conduct these company convoys to assembly
positions mentioned in 3(f).

Small spaces left in the gunners compartment will
be utilized for storing such rations as are
available.

One Officer from each company will report to
Lieutenant King[25] to conduct gas and ration truck from
NEUVILLE to assembly points mentioned in 3(f). Orders
for contents of these trucks have previously been given.
After emptying, these trucks will return immediately for
another load and return to the same point. Company
Commanders will detail one runner to remain at these
points and conduct trucks to new positions in case of
farther advance the following day.

5. Liaison.

(a) Infantry axis of liaison will be used. These
axes for the 28th and 35th Divisions are shown on
tracings furnished [not found with diary collection]

The Commanding Officer, Company "B" will send, by
these means, the following messages:

> One on D day at 12:00 Noon
> "   " "   "   "   4:00 p.m.
> "   " D plus 1 day at 7:00 a.m.
> "   " "   "   "   "   " 12:00 Noon
> "   " "   "   "   "   " 4:00 p.m.

The messages will be addressed to TANK LIAISON
OFFICER, 1st CORPS and will include statements of
casualties in men and material in addition to
general situation report.

---

[25] First Lieutenant Roswell King, Tank Corps.

(b) <u>PIGEONS</u> - Four pigeons will be detailed to each company. They should be used for reporting only pertinent incidents of the battle. All pigeons not previously released will be released on the night of D plus 1 day.

(c) P.C.'s. - 1st Brigade at P.C. of 35th Division in BOIS de FORIMONT.

344th Battalion (same as Brigade)

Representative of both Brigade and 344th Battalion Commander will be at QUARRY 800 M. south of VRAINCOURT.

SERENO E. BRETT.

Major, Tank Corps.

DATE: September 25, 1918

AVAILABLE FOR ALL DUTY: 46 Officers and 609 Men

WEATHER: Cloudy **ROADS:** Fair **HEALTH:** Good

CAMP: Good

NARRATIVE OF OPERATIONS:

The 344th continuing preparations for the attack. Battalion Field Order #2 issued. Tanks left lying-in position by companies 6:00 p.m. to 8:00 p.m. and arrived at respective positions at 12:30 a.m., September 26. Company B to support 28th Division position in readiness at ABANCOURT FARM. Companies A and C position in readiness 400 meters north of southwest corner LES COTES DE FORIMONT, point 05.2-68, map ARGONNE-MONTFAUCON 1:50,000.

The 345th Battalion made reconnaissance and established liaison with commands pertaining to attack. At 7:00 p.m. the battalion left lying-in position and moved to positions in readiness. Companies B and C east of AIRE RIVER at 04.2-68.0 arriving at 11:00 p.m. Company A west of AIRE RIVER at 03.2-67.8 arriving at 10:00 p.m.

Temporary Battalion Command Post in dug out COTES DE FORIMONT at 05.3-67.55.

The 4th French Army west of the ARGONNE FOREST began artillery preparation at 11:00 p.m.

DATE: September 26, 1918
AVAILABLE FOR ALL DUTY: 46 Officers and 607 Men
WEATHER: Fog-Fair **ROADS:** Poor **HEALTH:** Good
CAMP: Poor **LOSSES:** 1 Officer killed and 5 Officers
wounded; 4 Men wounded

NARRATIVE OF OPERATIONS:

This was "D" Day, "H" Hour at 5:30 a.m. A heavy fog lay over the area and did not lift until 10:00 a.m. Early in the morning Lieutenant Colonel G.S. Patton, Jr., Brigade Commander was wounded. At Colonel Patton's message request (copy attached)[26] Major S. E. Brett was placed in command of the brigade.

Companies A and C, 344th Battalion and Companies B and C, 345th Battalion operating with the 35th Division on the right bank of the AIRE RIVER. Company B, 344th Battalion and Company A, 345th Battalion operating with the 28th Division on the left bank of the RIVER AIRE.

Shortly after the attack started, the 344th Battalion and the 345th Battalion became merged into a forward group of tanks commanded by Captain Compton of the 345th Battalion, Major Brett as Brigade Commander remaining at command post at point 04.8-72.0 map ARGONNE-MONTFAUCON 1:50,000.

In the course of the day's fighting, very stubborn resistance was encountered and severe losses incurred by both tanks and infantry. Numerous machine gun nests and anti-tank guns were put out of action. The tanks assisted greatly in the capture of VARENNES, CHEPPY and VERY, entering all three towns several times before the infantry came up and occupied them. Cooperation between the tanks and infantry was, in most cases, very poor.

The 344th Battalion rallied and spent the night at VERY.

The 345th Battalion rallied and spent the night near VERY.

---

[26] Not found with archived diary collection.

DATE: September 27, 1918
AVAILABLE FOR ALL DUTY: 49 Officers and 608 Men
WEATHER: Rain **ROADS:** Poor **HEALTH:** Good
CAMP: Poor **LOSSES:** 1 Officer wounded; 4 Men killed and 3 Men wounded

NARRATIVE OF OPERATIONS:

Orders from Major Brett, acting Brigade Commander, placed Captain Compton in command of all tanks at the front, which included the 14th and 17th Groups French Tanks and the 344th and 345th Battalion Tank Corps.

Captain Compton placed Captain Barnard in command of the Companies A and C, 344th Battalion, and Companies B and C, 345th Battalion, operating on the east bank of the RIVER AIRE. Lieutenant Brown[27] was placed in Command of Company B, 344th Battalion, and Company A, 345th Battalion, operating on the west bank of the RIVER AIRE.

The French Groups operating on the east bank.

Captain Compton established command post at VARENNES (03.5-73.4). The tanks operating on the east bank of the AIRE RIVER moved out from VERY in three groups, Company A, 344th Battalion entering CHARPENTRY. Only small gains were made during the day, the infantry consolidating their lines on the plateau north of VERY.

On the west of the AIRE RIVER, Company B, 344th Battalion and Company A, 345th Battalion operated against FORET D'ARGONNE and aided the infantry to take LA FORGE FERME (02.6-75.3) and MONTBLAINVILLE (02.0-75.7)

Lieutenants Higgins, Llewellyn[28] and Gibbs with 15 tanks reported for duty from detached service.

Major Chanoine reports at 11:00 p.m. that he would have to withdraw on the 28th.

Brigade Command Post moved to COTES DE FORIMONT.

---

[27] First Lieutenant Thomas G. Brown.
[28] First Lieutenant Robert C. Llewellyn.

DATE: September 28, 1918
AVAILABLE FOR ALL DUTY: 42 Officers and 597 Men
WEATHER: Cloudy **ROADS:** Poor **HEALTH:** Good
CAMP: Poor **LOSSES:** 6 Officers wounded; 5 Men killed and 30 Men wounded

NARRATIVE OF OPERATIONS:

Captain Barnard with 40 tanks moved against BAULNY and CHAUDRON and SERIEUX FERME and occupied the ground to the east and west of MONTREBEAU WOODS but the infantry did not follow. Tanks retired to CHARPENTRY and VERY for the night.

The group on the west of the AIRE RIVER, under Lieutenant Brown, operated against the FOREST D'ARGONNE and at noon entered town of APREMONT but the infantry did not follow. The tanks retired to a ravine 800 meters south of APREMONT. Owing to heavy machine gun fire, the tanks once more entered the town and then fell back to the infantry lines.

About sundown, the infantry was ordered to follow the tanks. The tanks and infantry took APREMONT. After tanks remained at APREMONT and the balance returned to MONTBLAINVILLE for the night.

The French Groups reorganized after the capture of CHARPENTRY, but were relieved from further duty as their tanks and personnel were in bad condition.

The 376th and 377th Training and Replacement Companies arrived at CAMP FOURGOUS and were assigned to duty with 321st Repair and Salvage Company per V.O.C.O. Chief of Tank Corps.

DATE: September 29, 1918
AVAILABLE FOR ALL DUTY: 41 Officers and 574 Men
WEATHER: Cloudy **ROADS:** Poor **HEALTH:** Good
CAMP: Poor **LOSSES:** 1 Man killed and 4 Men wounded

NARRATIVE OF OPERATIONS:

Captain English left BAULNY and entered EXERMONT (01.7-80.9) but was unable to hold it as the infantry gave no support. He retired to BAULNY for the night.

Confusion among the infantry caused them to retire slightly giving up some small gains. Tanks sent in by orders from Captain Compton, near MONTREBEAU, aided the infantry to restore the old line.

Lieutenants Brown, Gibbs and Roy[29] attempted to work north of APREMONT but found it impossible due to heavy artillery fire.

Tanks were held in readiness for a counterattack.

DATE: September 30, 1918
AVAILABLE FOR ALL DUTY: 40 Officers and 557 Men
WEATHER: Rain **ROADS:** Poor **HEALTH:** Good
CAMP: Poor

NARRATIVE OF OPERATIONS:

Captain English and Lieutenant Grant[30] were ordered to move to CHARPENTRY with tanks. At 8:00 a.m. 35th Division requested tanks to ward off counterattack northeast of ECLISFONTAINE (05.8-78.0). Twenty-four tanks were deployed at SERIEUX FERME. No attack developed and after four hours, tanks withdrew to prepare for an attack on MONTREBEAU WOODS (01.5-79.5). Attack order was rescinded.

At 6:00 p.m. message was received that 1st Division was to relieve the 35th Division and tanks prepared to attack with them the next day. All tanks east of the RIVER AIRE were consolidated at CHARPENTRY. The group west of the RIVER AIRE was held in readiness all day at APREMONT.

Later in the morning the 35th Division again requested tanks to ward off counterattack developing north of CHARPENTRY. Twenty tanks were dispatched and deployed but no counterattack developed.

---

[29] Second Lieutenant John W. Roy.
[30] Second Lieutenant Gordon M. Grant.

PATTON WAR DIARY - OCTOBER 1918

October 1918.
304TH (1st) Brigade
Tank Corps

This book is for one month;
do not tear out sheets.

WAR DIARY INSTRUCTIONS

1. Observe F. S. R., Paragraph 35.

2. This is the HISTORY of what your unit accomplishes, in other words, of OPERATIONS. Tell what actually happened; not what is supposed to have happened. Abstain from criticism.

3. Append all orders, messages, plans, sketches, etc.

4. Designate precisely each place and position occupied; assume that the reader never heard of any of them.

5. Note the personnel, losses and statistics of unit as changes occur; give dates, hours, state of weather, atmosphere and roads.

6. Enter the higher units to which you belong: brigades, divisions, corps, etc.

7. When maneuvering, always try to get the designations and positions of units next to you in line.

8. Tactical observations are particularly desired.

9. No erasures may be made in this Diary.

10. The C. O. must sign before the return is made at the end of the calendar month.

A. E. Printing Dept., G. H. Q. A. E. F., 1918.

Col. J. C.

Image of cover to Patton's War Diary for October 1918.

DATE: October 1, 1918
AVAILABLE FOR ALL DUTY: 34 Officers and 608 Men
WEATHER: Cloudy **ROADS:** Fair **HEALTH:** Good
CAMP: Fair **LOSSES:** 3 Men killed and 13 Men wounded
[Notes at left margin of diary page:
"Tuesday Maps. Foret d'Argonne Verdun 1/20000.
Operating with 91st Division Right, 1st Division Center,
28th Division Left."]

NARRATIVE OF OPERATIONS:

Tanks reported for action this date 61.

28th Division requested group of eight tanks to cooperate in attack scheduled at 6:00 a.m. The enemy attacked at 5:30 a.m. The tanks were in position and did terrible execution to the massed ranks of the enemy, in addition to capturing two officers and 26 men.

Brigadier General Nolan[1] of the 28th Division personally commended them for their valuable work. Sergeant Dutt, Corporal Whitney and Private Casey were killed. Five tanks were completely wrecked.

Summary of intelligence 1st Army Corps dated October 2nd states relative to the action: prisoners of the 2nd Landwehr Division state that in the counterattack north of APREMONT they were entirely demoralized by our tanks as most of their soldiers had never seen tanks before.

After doing effective work going through the lines the tanks returned inflicting heavy losses as they passed. Two tanks patrolling on the APREMONT-LE-MENIL FERME ROAD (98.6-78.6) met slight resistance and returned to their positions after having accomplished their missions.

Repair and salvage being splendidly handled by Lieutenant Thompson[2] but is becoming more difficult due to the proximity of disabled tanks to the enemy's lines.

---

[1] Brigadier General Dennis E. Nolan.
[2] First Lieutenant Jesse L. Thompson, T.C., 316th Company (R & S – American).

G.H.Q.
American Expeditionary Forces
Special Orders)   France, Oct. 2, 1918.
No. 275   )
                    EXTRACT
        1. Under the provisions of G.O. No. 78, War
Department, 1918, the following temporary
appointments in the Tank Corps, United States Army,
during the existing emergency, are announced, with
rank from October 2, 1918: [All assigned to perform
"present duties."]

NAME   APPOINTED
                    From   To
Frank G. Nelson   Sgt.1cl.   2nd Lieut.
Jerome V. Fite   Sgt.1cl.   2nd Lieut.
George A. Work   Sgt.1cl.   2nd Lieut.
Arthur Snyder   Sgt.   2nd Lieut.
Donald M. Taylor   Sgt.   2nd Lieut.
Donald M. Call   Cpl.   2nd Lieut.
John C. Leathem   Cpl.   2nd Lieut.
William E. Phelps   Cpl.   2nd Lieut.

        Pending the confirmation of these appointments
and the receipt of commissions from the War
Department this order will serve the purpose of a
commission.
            By Command of General PERSHING:
                        JAMES W. McANDREW
                        Chief of Staff

ADVANCED HEADQUARTERS FIRST ARMY CORPS
                Oct. 2, 1918.
From: Chief of Staff, 1st Army Corps, U.S.
To: Commanding Officer, 1st Tank Brigade, U.S.
Subject: Assignment of tanks for operations
contemplated by Field Orders No. 63.
        1. The Corps Commander directs that for the
operations now pending you assign two companies of
tanks to be utilized in the front of the 1st
Division.
        2. One company of tanks will be assigned to
the front of the 28th Division.
        3. The remaining company will follow in
support, with a view of being utilized on the front

of the 28th Division when the front as the Division advances becomes wide enough for the operations of the additional company.

4. You will direct the proper company commanders to establish liaison with the Division, Commanders to which assigned with a view to being in place and starting at the proper time.

By command of Major General Liggett:

MALIN CRAIG
Chief of Staff.

––––––––––

DATE: October 2, 1918
AVAILABLE FOR ALL DUTY: 34 Officers and 591 Men
WEATHER: Rain **ROADS:** Fair **HEALTH:** Good **CAMP:** Fair
LOSSES: 12 Men wounded
[Notes at left margin of diary page:
"Wednesday Maps. Foret d'Argonne Verdun 1/20000.
Operating with 91st Division Right, 1st Division Center,
28th Division Left."]

NARRATIVE OF OPERATIONS:

Number of tanks ready for action this date 69.

No action during day.

Tanks remained in position in reserve near CHARPENTRY-MONTBLAINVILLE in compliance with Field Orders #61-62-63 1st Army Corps.

Detachment of 103rd Engineers on duty with brigade at VARENNES relieved and directed to report to their original organization per S.O. #2-1st Tank Brigade October 2nd 1918.

DATE: October 3, 1918
AVAILABLE FOR ALL DUTY: 33 Officers and 589 men
WEATHER: Cloudy **ROADS:** Fair **HEALTH:** Good
CAMP: Fair **LOSSES:** 1 Man wounded
[Notes at left margin of diary page:
"Thursday Maps. Foret d'Argonne Verdun 1/20000.
Operating with 91st Division Right, 1st Division Center,
28th Division Left."]

NARRATIVE OF OPERATIONS:

Number of tanks ready for action this date 89.

Tanks remained in reserve near CHARPENTRY and BAULNY. One tank was struck by gas shell tearing off the turret and wounding two men. Eighteen tanks replaced today by the repair and salvage.

Disposition for October 4th - two companies to support the advance of the 28th Division. One additional company in support echelon.

Telegram received from G.H.Q. announcing temporary appointments as second lieutenants, Tank Corps (copy attached).

Conference called at the respective command posts and problem fully discussed.

Work and cooperation with 1st Division most satisfactory.

DATE: October 4, 1918
ORGANIZATION: Companies A and C, 344th Battalion; Companies B and C, 345th Battalion
FROM: Baulny-Serieux Ferme **TO:** Fleville-Cote 240
DISTANCE: 5 kilometers
ORGANIZATION: Company, 344th Battalion; Company A, 345th Battalion **FROM:** Apremont **TO:** Chatel Chehery
DISTANCE: 3 kilometers
AVAILABLE FOR ALL DUTY: 32 Officers and 582 Men
WEATHER: Cloudy **ROADS:** Fair **HEALTH:** Good
CAMP: Fair **LOSSES:** 1 Officer killed and 2 Officers wounded; [2 or 5 – unclear because numbers written over each other] Men killed and 6 Men wounded
[Notes at left margin of diary page:
"Friday Maps. Foret d'Argonne Verdun 1/20000.
Operating with 32nd Division Right, 1st Division Center, 28th Division Left, 77th Division Left."]
NARRATIVE OF OPERATIONS:
Tanks ready for action 89.

Disposition of the tanks for the attack on this date was as follows:

Two companies to the 1st Division.

One company to the 35th Division.

Remaining tanks were retained in position as brigade reserve until 2:00 p.m. at which hour a group of 13 tanks moved forward in rear of the 1st Division. These were intended for replacements at the end of the day and did not enter the action.

The tanks went over at H-hour (5:30 a.m.) in the face of a most determined resistance, it being a renewal of the main offensive begun the 26th of September. Tank work was reported by the infantry as being most effective.

Severe work developed for the tanks near HILL 240 (01-82) in the sector of the 1st Division and along the east edge of the FORET D'ARGONNE in the sector of the 28th Division. The brigade reserve of 13 tanks left VARENNES at 2:00 p.m. and followed the advance of the 1st Division.

Casualties in both tanks and personnel were extremely heavy. Captain English, Lieutenant Llewellyn and four enlisted men were killed, Lieutenants Phillips,[3] Gleason,[4] Wood,[5] Sewall,[6] Morrison,[7] McCluer and Nelms[8] were wounded and many casualties among the enlisted men.

Spirit of men and officers excellent but tanks are in very poor mechanical condition. The enemy artillery and hundreds of machine guns set up in the FORET D'ARGONNE made the taking of LE CHENE TONDU (99.5-76.8) extremely difficult for tanks and infantry.

---

[3] Second Lieutenant Darwin T. Phillips.

[4] Second Lieutenant J. W. Gleason.

[5] Either Second Lieutenant E. E. or H. A. Wood. Both are listed on Tank Corps organization roster as assigned to the 326th (344th) Battalion as of September 10, 1918. See Rockenbach, p. 78.

[6] First Lieutenant Loyall F. Sewall.

[7] Second Lieutenant Julian K. Morrison.

[8] First Lieutenant Horace C. Nelms.

DATE: October 5, 1918
ORGANIZATION: Company A, 345th Battalion
FROM: Chatel Chehery **TO:** Near Cote 180
DISTANCE: 2.5 kilometers
AVAILABLE FOR ALL DUTY: 29 Officers and 571 Men
WEATHER: Cloudy **ROADS:** Fair **HEALTH:** Good
CAMP: Fair **LOSSES:** 1 Officer killed and I Officer wounded;
26 Men wounded
[Notes at left margin of diary page:
"Saturday Maps. Foret d'Argonne Verdun 1/20000.
Operating with 32nd Division Right, 1st Division Center,
28th Division Left, 77th Division Left."]
NARRATIVE OF OPERATIONS:
Tanks ready for action 30.

Disposal of tanks as follows:

15 to the 1st Division.

15 to the 28th Division.

Neither of the divisions to which tanks were assigned called for them during the day. Tanks moved up to close support of the divisions and after dark returned to their positions. Mechanical troubles in tanks are becoming more numerous each day. This is due to the fact that the tanks have been under severe test both in the ST. MIHIEL and the present offensive. The above troubles are seriously hampering our operations.

The men and officers are in good spirits. Nightly gassing of our positions has caused a little sickness and inconvenience.

By arrangement with the 1st Army Corps all tanks were withdrawn to reserve positions near CHARPENTRY and MONTBLAINVILLE and no tanks were to be used except on instructions from the Corps.

Summary of intelligence 1st Army Corps this date state that on examination of 14 prisoners the following was learned: "Yesterday morning October 4th 1918 at 11:30 a.m. they were alarmed and told that the Americans had broken through and that they must counterattack. They left immediately and marched around the western side of HILL 240. The 2nd Foot Guard followed them and they went into line at 300.8-281.5 from the above point but as they did the tanks came toward them and drove them back. Most of the men so the prisoners stated returned into the woods."

Per instructions H.Q. 1st Army Corps time was set back one hour at midnight October 5th-6th.

DATE: October 6, 1918
AVAILABLE FOR ALL DUTY: 26 Officers and 562 Men
WEATHER: Rain **ROADS:** Good **HEALTH:** Fair **CAMP:** Fair
LOSSES: [2 or 3] Officers wounded [numbers written over each other]; 1 Man killed and 13 Men wounded
[Notes at left margin of diary page:
"Sunday Maps. Foret d'Argonne [sic] 1/20000.
Operating with 32nd Division Right, 1st Division Center,
28th Division Left, 77th Division Left."]
NARRATIVE OF OPERATIONS:
Tanks ready for action this date 17.

Under direction of 1st Army Corps they were held in reserve.

No fighting was done by the tanks but 24 were made ready for action the next day.

1st Army Corps ordered one company of tanks to the support of the 28th Division October 7th. The tanks were in bad condition as under the conditions it was impossible to do any thorough overhauling. About two platoons were held on each side of the river in readiness for an emergency call.

DATE: October 7, 1918
AVAILABLE FOR ALL DUTY: 24 Officers and 534 Men
WEATHER: Rain **ROADS:** Good **HEALTH:** Good
CAMP: Fair **LOSSES:** 4 Men wounded
[Notes at left margin of diary page:
"Monday Maps. Foret d'Argonne Verdun 1/20000.
Operating with 32nd Division Right, 1st Division Center,
28th Division Left, 77th Division Left."]
NARRATIVE OF OPERATIONS:
Only eight tanks were available to support the 28th Division. These were dispatched. One hit a mine north of APREMONT and was disabled. The remaining seven tanks

reported later and were used throughout the day for patrol work.

Five tanks are in good condition and 21 in such condition that one day's fighting only can be expected.

DATE: October 8, 1918
AVAILABLE FOR ALL DUTY: 23 Officers and 518 Men
WEATHER: Rain **ROADS:** Good **HEALTH:** Fair **CAMP:** Fair
LOSSES: 8 Men wounded
[Notes at left margin of diary page:
"Tuesday Maps. Foret d'Argonne Verdun 1/20000.
Operating with 32nd Division Right, 1st Division Center,
82nd Division Left, 77th Division Left."]
NARRATIVE OF OPERATIONS:
Tanks ready for action this date 26.

The left group of seven tanks assigned to 28th Division.

Twenty-four tanks reported in Repair Park, 12 of which were in running order and 12 requiring extensive repairs. A great many evacuations among the personnel on account of sickness.

Command post 1st Brigade moved from COTES DE FORIMONT to VARENNES.

DATE: October 9, 1918
AVAILABLE FOR ALL DUTY: 23 Officers and 516 Men
WEATHER: Rain **ROADS:** Good **HEALTH:** Fair **CAMP:** Fair
[Notes at left margin of diary page:
"Wednesday Maps. Foret d'Argonne Verdun 1/20000.
Operating with 32nd Division Right, 1st Division Center,
28th, 82nd, 77th Divisions Left."]
NARRATIVE OF OPERATIONS:
Tanks ready for action this date 35.

The above tanks were placed at the disposal of the 82nd Division which had replaced the 28th. The tanks were not called for during the day.

All personnel engaged in making repairs.

Instructions from Chief of Staff, 1st Army Corps to hold all tanks in reserve during the 10th October. Commanding Officer of Repair and Salvage directed to evacuate all disabled tanks from the CHARPENTRY-MONTBLAINVILLE area to the VARENNES area, the battalion repair units to be employed in the work.

Captain Compton moved his command post to MONTBLAINVILLE.

Major Brett moved his command post to VARENNES.

DATE: October 10, 1918
AVAILABLE FOR ALL DUTY: 19 Officers and 498 Men
WEATHER: Rain **ROADS:** Good **HEALTH:** Fair **CAMP:** Fair
LOSSES: 1 Officer wounded; 2 Men wounded
[Notes at left margin of diary page:
"Thursday Maps. Foret d'Argonne Verdun 1/20000.
Operating with 32nd Division Right, 1st Division Center,
77th, 82nd Divisions Left."]
NARRATIVE OF OPERATIONS:
No action. Tanks remained in same location. Fifty-eight tanks in park at VARENNES; 39 running, 17 being repaired, 2 salvaged.

Captain Compton directed to hold available tanks at MONTBLAINVILLE during the 11th. Instructions from the 1st Army Corps to the effect that two companies would be employed on October 11th.

All personnel both mechanical and combatant were put on the two companies of tanks which were given special mechanical attention.

GENERAL HEADQUARTERS – TANK CORPS
AMERICAN EXPEDITIONARY FORCES
11th October, 1918.
GENERAL ORDERS)
No. 17   )
     1. The following provisional organization of Tank Corps Troops is announced:
     1st Brigade: Lt. Colonel G.S. Patton, Jr. T.C., Commanding, Headquarters 1st Brigade, 321st Company, 344th Battalion, 328th Battalion and 303rd Battalion.
     2nd Brigade: Lt. Colonel H.E. Mitchell, T.C., Commanding, Headquarters 2nd Brigade, 306th Company,

301st Battalion, 329th Battalion and 330th
Battalion.
     3rd Brigade: Lt. Colonel D.D. Pullen, T.C.,
Commanding, Headquarters 3rd Brigade, 316th Company,
302nd Provisional Battalion, 345th Battalion and
331st Battalion.
     2. The heavy battalions and training center
now with the British will join on or about the 1st
of November.
     3. Lt. Colonel G.S. Patton, Jr., T.C. is
relieved as Commandant of the 302nd Center, Tank
Corps and Major Joseph Viner detailed in his stead.
     4. The temporary home station of the 1st, 2nd
and 3rd Brigades is the 302nd Center, Tank Corps.
The Commandant will assign camps and billets and
make schedule for using the training facilities.
     By Command of Brigadier General Rockenbach:
          GEORGE J.CROSBY
          Captain, Tank Corps,
          Adjutant.

DATE: October 11, 1918
ORGANIZATION: Company C, 345th Battalion
FROM: Varennes **TO:** Fleville **DISTANCE:** 12 kilometers
AVAILABLE FOR ALL DUTY: 93 Officers and 1346 Men
WEATHER: Cloudy **ROADS:** Good **HEALTH:** Fair
CAMP: Fair
[Notes at left margin of diary page:
"Friday Maps. Foret d'Argonne [sic] 1/20000.
Operating with 32nd Division Right, 1st Division Center,
77th, 82nd Divisions Left."]
NARRATIVE OF OPERATIONS:

Number of tanks reported in condition this date 48.

Twenty-three tanks left VARENNES at 12 midnight
October 10-11 to comply with V.O.C.O. Chief of Staff, 1st
Army Corps.

Due to mechanical troubles only three of them reported
at FLEVILLE. Those three reported to the Commanding
General, 164th Brigade, 82nd Division but were rejected
because three instead of five, as had been requested,
reported.

Group of five tanks operating with the 77th Division reported at PYLONE but were not called for during the day.

Instructions received from Chief of Tank Corps relative to future operations containing directions to organize a provisional company. Copy attached.[9]

Received copy of G.O. #17, General Tank Headquarters October 11th 1918, making provisional organization of Tank Corps troops. Three brigades to be organized, each made up of one headquarters company, one repair and salvage company, two battalions light tanks, one battalion heavy tanks.

344th Battalion assigned to 1st Brigade, Lieutenant Colonel George S. Patton Jr. commanding Brigade and relieved from command of 302nd Tank Center. Tanks and personnel to assemble at VARENNES for organization.

The 304th Tank Brigade now consists of:

321st Repair & Salvage Co.	1 Officer	53 Men
344th Battalion	6 Officers	196 Men
328th Battalion	15 Officers	320 Men
303rd Battalion	71 Officers	777 Men
Total	93 Officers	1346 Men

The 328th Battalion is at the 302nd Center, BOURG, France; the 303rd Battalion at NEUVY-PAILLOUX, France. 301st Center and the 344th Battalion less three officers and 94 enlisted men returning to the 302nd Center.

```
        Headquarters First Division
        American Expeditionary Forces,
          France, October 12, 1918
From:    Chief of Staff, 1st Division
To:      Commanding Officer, 1st Brigade Tanks
Subject: Appreciation of services.
     1. The Commanding General, 1st Division,
directs me to express to you his appreciation and
the appreciation of the officers and men of this
```

---

[9] Not attached. However, see "Condition of Provisional Company," the manning roster for the provisional company, immediately following the October 13 diary entry.

PATTON WAR DIARY - OCTOBER 1918

division for the assistance given by the 1st Brigade
Tanks to the 1st Division during the operations
between the ARGONNE and the MEUSE, September 29th to
October 11th, inclusive.
     2. The willingness and energy shown by all
detachments of the 1st Brigade Tanks operating with
the 1st Division were worthy of the best traditions
of the service, but only what the 1st Division
expects of the 1st Brigade Tanks.
                   J. N. Greely
                   Chief of Staff

———————

DATE: October 12, 1918
AVAILABLE FOR ALL DUTY: 93 Officers and 1345 Men
WEATHER: Rain **ROADS:** Good **HEALTH:** Fair **CAMP:** Fair
[Notes at left margin of diary page:
"Saturday Maps. Foret d'Argonne 1/20000.
Operating with 32nd Division Right, 1st Division Center,
77th Division Left."]
NARRATIVE OF OPERATIONS:

Tanks and personnel continued assembling at
VARENNES.

Letter received from Chief of Staff for Commanding
General, 1st Division commending 1st Brigade Tank Corps
on its splendid work. Copy attached.

Details of organizing the Provisional Company were
pushed.

Captain Compton was relieved by Major Brett of the
command of the forward tanks and again took command of
the 345th Battalion.

The 303rd Battalion stationed at WORGRET CAMP,
WAREHAM, DORSET, ENGLAND is receiving English
instruction in Heavy Tank Warfare consisting of tank
sequence, gunnery sequence, camouflage, pigeon
reconnaissance and mechanical school.

The 328th Battalion stationed at CAMP CHAMBERLAIN-BOURG, FRANCE is being intensively trained in the following:

1. Tank School
    a. Shop Work
    b. Gas Engine
    c. Tank Driving
2. Field School
    a. Visibility
    b. Messages
    c. Signaling
3. Pistol-Grenades
4. Machine Gun
5. 37mm Gun

Attached is a sample schedule for a week and a list of drill calls.

PATTON WAR DIARY - OCTOBER 1918

TRAINING SCHEDULE

DAYS	MONDAY			TUESDAY			WEDNESDAY			THURSDAY			FRIDAY			SATURDAY			SUN
PERIODS	1	2	3	1	2	3	1	2	3	1	2	3	1	2	3	1	2	3	1
Co."A"				Guard & Fatigue			7	8	9	4	5	6	1	2	3	Guard & Fatigue			
Co."B"				Field Training			8	9	7	7	8	9	2	3	1	Field Training			
Co."C"				By Bn. C.O.			9	7	8	9	7	8	3	1	2	By Bn. C.O.			
Co."A"				1	2	3	Guard & Fatigue			Guard & Fatigue			4	5	6	1	2	3	
Co."B"				2	3	1	Field Training			Field Training			5	6	4	2	3	1	
Co."C"				3	1	2	By Bn. C.O			By Bn. C.O.			6	4	5	3	1	2	
Co."A"				4	5	6	1	2	3	1	2	3	6	4	5	4	5	6	
Co."B"				5	6	4	2	3	1	2	3	1	7	8	9	5	6	4	
Co."C"				6	4	5	3	1	2	3	1	2	8	9	7	6	4	5	
Co."A"				7	8	9	4	5	6	1	2	3	Guard & Fatigue			7	8	9	
Co."B"				8	9	7	5	6	4	2	3	1	Field Training			8	9	7	
Co."C"				9	7	8	6	4	5	3	1	2	By Bn. C.O			9	7	3	

325th Batt'n   326th Batt'n   330th Battalion   331st Battalion

1st PERIOD 7:30 A.M. - 9:30 A.M.: 2nd PERIOD 9:45 A.M. - 11:45 A.M.: 3rd PERIOD 1:00 P.M. - 3:00 P.M.

CAMP HEADQUARTERS
302nd TANK CENTER

The following list of Calls will become effective October
12th, 1918, for all members of this command.

	Week days except Saturdays	Saturdays	Hollidays
REVEILLE			
First Call	5:50	5:50	
Reveille	6:00	6:00	
Assembly	6:05	6:05	
Moss (Breakfast)	6:45	6:45	7:45
Sick Call	7:00	7:00	8:00
SCHOOL AND FATIGUE			
School Call	7:20	7:20	
Assembly	7:30	7:30	
Fatigue Call	7:20	7:20	
Assembly	7:2 5	7:25	
Recall from School	9:30	9:30	
Assembly from School	9:45	9:45	
1st Sgts. Call	11:30	11:30	11:30
Recall from School	11:45	11:45	
Recall from Fatigue	11:45	11:45	
Mess (Dinner)	12:00	12:00	
SCHOOL AND FATIGUE			
School Call	12:50		
Assembly	1:00		
Fatigue Call	12:50		
Assembly	12:55		
Recall from School	3:00		
Recall from Fatigue	4:30		
GUARD MOUNTING			
Guard Mount	4:35	4:35	4:35
Assembly	4:40	4:40	4:40
RETREAT			
First Call	4:45		
Assembly	4:55		
Retreat	5:00		
Moss (Supper)	5:15	5:15	5:15
TATOO	9:00	9:00	9:00
CALL TO QUARTERS	9:45	9:45	9:45
TAPS	10:00	10:00	10:00

BY ORDER OF CAPT. CALHOUN:

FRANK G. NELSON
2nd Lt. T.C., U.S.A
Ass't. Adjt.

Images of sample "Training Schedule" (previous page) and "List of Drill Calls" (this
page) cited in Patton's October 12 entry and affixed to adjacent pages of diary.

GUNNERY SCHOOL

```
        ( Nomenclat ure & Functioning
        ( Dismounting and assembling
  M. G  ( Sighting
        ( Jams - Stoppages
        (           (Elementary
        ( Fireing   (Advanced


        ( Nomenclature & Functioning
        ( Sighting
  37MM  (           ( Elementary
        ( Fireing   ( Advanced
```

PISTOL - GRENADES

Field School

Visibility - Patrols - Target Designation.

Messages - Runners - Liaison Agents.

Signalling - Wig-wag - semaphore - Pigeon.

TANK   School

```
                  ( Nomenclature
  Shop  Work      ( Oiling
                  ( Minor repairs
                  ( Motor Trouble

                  ( Theory of Engine - carburet or - magneto
  Gas Engine      (  etc.
                  (

                  ( Jacked up Tank.
  Tank Driving    ( Field Driving ( Elementary
                  (               ( Advanced
                  ( Trench Driving
```

Image of list of training also found affixed adjacent to Patton's October 12 entry.

DATE: October 13, 1918
AVAILABLE FOR ALL DUTY: 95 Officers and 1344 Men
WEATHER: Rain **ROADS:** Good **HEALTH:** Fair **CAMP:** Fair
[Notes at left margin of diary page:
"Sunday Maps. Foret d'Argonne 1/20000.
Operating with 32nd Division Right, 1st Division Center,
77th Division Left."]
NARRATIVE OF OPERATIONS:

First Provisional Tank Company organized per Order #1, Headquarters 1st Tank Brigade. Copy attached.[10]

Personnel of Provisional Tank Company, made up of 10 officers and 149 enlisted men, a total of 159, drawn from the six companies of the 344th and 345th Battalions.[11] Equipment of Provisional Company progressing. Salvaging of tanks in forward areas continuing.

Captain Compton relieved of command of forward group and returned to command of 345th Battalion which now started to move by truck and automobile to BOURG.

Provisional Company to relieve the forward group. Equipment of Provisional Company as follows: twenty-four tanks, one Dodge car, four trucks, one motorcycle with side car, one rolling kitchen, one water wagon.

```
       CONDITION OF PROVISIONAL COMPANY, 1ST BRIGADE.
                    OFFICERS PRESENT.
              Captain C.H. Barnard
              First Lieutenant John W. Fordyce
              First Lieutenant Henry C. Jennings
              Second Lieutenant Floyd Callahan
              Second Lieutenant W.M. Louisell
              Second Lieutenant Churchill C. Peters
```

---

[10] Not found with archived diary.

[11] "Condition of Provisional Company, 1st Brigade," roster of officers and men appended to the diary differs slightly in its numbers. See roster immediately following this diary entry. Listed in the roster are only six officers and 140 Men, not counting the four Men evacuated.

ENLISTED MEN PRESENT.

Company "A" 344th Battalion

Sergeant First Class Appleby, 83155 Joseph W.
Sergeant Barnes, 243396 Marvin A.
    "   Casey, 243406 James A.
    "   Magill, 78287 John
    "   White, 243380 Edward J.
Corporal Mousoe, 237616 Jacob
    "   Peters, 2392717 Wayne S.
    "   Sunberg, 136764 Paul V.
Private Colmerauer, 243408 Maurice A.
    "   Everett, 123458 Henry B.
    "   Joh, 243435 Frederick C.
    "   Son, 178983 Harvey
    "   Stephens, 2390698 Paul J.
    "   Thompson, 148520 Clarence
    "   Wardell, 152500 Richard

Company "B" 344th Battalion

Sergeant First Class Martinnetti, 243472 Thomas
Sergeant Adams, 218047 Max S.
    "   Hay, 243563 Kenneth A.
    "   Lohman, 700015 Earl C.
    "   Osland, 82719 Robert
    "   Selby, 139881 Keith
    "   Shelly, 28804 Clement H.
    "   Walls, 149158 Russell H.
Corporal Frederick, 721706 Linus
    "   Kelly, 8527 Edward E.
    "   Murphy, 72337 John E.
    "   Schuchneck, 139925 Leo
    "   Sutherland, 81240 Edward L.
    "   Williams, 178245 Austin R.
Private First Class Barnhardt, 139202 Lonzo H.
    "   "   "   Guggimos, 243470 Joseph
    "   "   "   Hansen, 84961 Herman E.
    "   "   "   Helton, 154959 Frank B.
    "   "   "   Hurtuk, 64887 Stephen H.
    "   "   "   Jettke, 18973 Harry H.
    "   "   "   Riggs, 1580065 Hugh M.
    "   "   "   Stitzer, 243551 Albert F.
    "   "   "   Spurgeon, 186356 Glen H.
    "   "   "   Whitman, (unknown)Alfred M.
    "   "   "   Yorke, 189439 Roswell G.
Private Deily, 243507 Eston A.

Company "C" 344th Battalion

Sergeant First Class Combs, 215429 Richard E.
Sergeant Berg, 254379 Harold R.
    "   Clapp, 71564 Roger H.
    "   Karolevitz, 140159 Frank B.
    "   Kuch, 127116 Allan
Cook   Jenkins, 140245 Frederick
Corporal Carmody, 140234 Martin J.
    "   Dent, 140152 Wilson M.
    "   Fahl, 259525 Ralph E.
    "   Pearson, 259749 Wilbur P.
    "   Ricou, 159394 Clarence A.
Private First Class Renick, 198586 Robert E.
Private   Adams, 218047 Francis E.
    "   Donnely, 137875 Albert A.
    "   Guy, 1590173 Charles R.
    "   Moore, 254402 George
    "   Neynaber, (unknown) Raymond A.
    "   Nichols, (unknown) John R.
    "   Swart, 85013 Floyd R.
    "   Walker, 139366 Edmund
    "   Weaver, 161480 Stanley C.

Company "A" 345th Battalion

Sergeant O'Brien, 243451 James P.
    "   Peterson, 243452 Roy C.
    "   Wheelock, 243377 Harry G.
    "   Young, 243375 Charles C.
Corporal Bell, 11558 Robert W.
    "   Branic, 169363 Archie C.
    "   Delisa, 243415 Joseph
    "   Garber, 135706 Jacob W.
    "   Haynie, 243429 Willard
    "   Jolin, 243430 Bertram
    "   Sutton, 70547 Clarence
Private First Class Hughes, 243432 Bert G.
    "   "   "   Pettey, 196945 Elliott W.
Private Bray, 84918 Thurman
    "   Ellis, 178828 Herman H.
    "   Heer, 679251 W.G. (could not locate on
        our roster)
    "   Nollerud, 2062675 Orville A.
    "   Smith, 178982 Earl A.
    "   Von Behren, 2964331 David C.
    "   Westervelt, 596560 Luther B.

<u>Company "B" 345th Battalion</u>
Sergeant Babcock, 136153 Horace H.
    "   Boulier, 243482 Frank A.
    "   Collins, 243491 Donald A.
    "   Elliott, 10609 Benjamin C.
    "   Everett 237477 James W.
Corporal Braden, 243488 William D.
    "   Breese, 243501 James A.
    "   Collmer, 10608 George R.
    "   Dilts, 243509 George W.
    "   Fink, 236902 Frank H.
    "   Iannarella, 243525 James V.
    "   Keating, 243484 Philip
    "   Lyon, 245443 Emery M.
    "   Richards, 243545 Claton
    "   Spalding, 10289 James F.
    "   Stauch, 243552 Robert F. A.W.O.L.
    "   Wieneke, 35868 Raemon H.
    "   Williams, 178245 Charles V.
Private First Class Anderson, 191021 Arthur
    "   "   "   Andrews, 343495 Robert E.
    "   "   "   Bittenbender,233499 Melvin C.
    "   "   "   Bogucki, 2423578 Ignatius
[Same serial number as Ellington, Lexton; so one of
them is incorrect.]
    "   "   "   Brooks, 1572005 Harold
    "   "   "   Ellington, 2423578 Lexton
    "   "   "   Flaugher, 1567888 Emery
    "   "   "   Leonard, 243530 Thomas A.
    "   "   "   McRorie, 259718 Clyde F.
    "   "   "   Regan, 2114862 Thomas B.
    "   "   "   Siffert, 204493 William H.
    "   "   "   Torgerson,1096608 Ralph T.
    "   "   "   Tucker, 1295659 John R.
    "   "   "   Wilson, 135766 James W.

<u>Company "C" 345th Battalion</u>
Sergeant Buckley, 241536 James J.
    "   Hedemark, 140140 Peter
    "   O'Farrell, 139307 Brendon
    "   Walden, 1937242 Alva A.

```
Corporal Burton, 140229 Bill
   "     Knudtson, 259869 John A.
   "     Moore, 22870 Charles C.
   "     Sicard, 140167 Felix
   "     Smith, 2337870 Mervin
   "     Stefanik, 259954 George
Private Biswell, 2214329 Elmore V.
   "     Bradley, 679344 Edward
   "     Burns, 73560 William F.
   "     Butler, 22889 John B.
   "     Childress, 15089 Melvin
   "     Gross, 15692 Earnest F.
   "     Keller, 20779 Joe
   "     Keykendall, 218752 James
   "     Mahoney, 679374 Raymond D.
   "     Mankin, 123869 Clinton
   "     Merritt, 170273 Charles V.
   "     Putney, 191215 Rodney I.
   "     Volk, 41403 Frank J.
   "     Whittaker, 136777 Fred
```

Headquarters Company

```
Private Kenworthy, 259780 William H.
   "     Landis, 155175 Wald E.
```

Men Evacuated

```
Sergeant Major 187614 Harland W.
Sergeant First Class Jones, 242233 Henry
Corporal Garwood, 214662 Guy W.
Private Roberts, 73693 Henry
```

HEADQUARTERS FIRST ARMY
AMERICAN EXPEDITIONARY FORCES, FRANCE
14 October 1918   15:10 Hours

SPECIAL ORDERS)
NO. 433   )

1. Pursuant to instructions of the C in C, A.E.F., the 1st Brigade Tank Corps (less Headquarters, 344th Battalion the 321st Company, and the Provisional Company) will withdraw to the 302d Tank Center, near LANGRES, for reorganization, replacements and training, reporting on arrival to the Center Commander.

2. Major Brett will remain in command of the advanced detachments.

3. All Tanks and the authorized transportation for the remaining units will be held, balance will be sent to Brigade Headquarters at 302d Center.

4. Movement will be started at once.
By command of General PERSHING:
H. A. DRUM
Chief of Staff

DATE: October 14, 1918
ORGANIZATION: 1st Provisional Company
FROM: Varennes **HOUR:** 7:00 p.m. **TO:** Exermont
HOUR: 10:00 p.m. **DISTANCE:** 5 kilometers
AVAILABLE FOR ALL DUTY: 94 Officers and 1343 Men
WEATHER: Rain **ROADS:** Good **HEALTH:** Good
CAMP: Fair

[Notes at left margin of diary page:
"Monday Maps. Foret d'Argonne 1/20000.
Operating with 42nd Division."]

NARRATIVE OF OPERATIONS:

The 1st Brigade Tank Corps, less Headquarters Company, 344th Battalion, the 321st Repair and Salvage Company, and the Provisional Company, was directed to withdraw to the 302nd Center Tank Corps, per S.O. 433 Headquarters 1st Army, dated October 14th, 1918. Copy attached.

During the evening of the 14th October the Provisional Company started to march to EXERMONT to be in readiness for action.

During the evening the Provisional Company was loaned to the 5th Army Corps by the 1st Army Corps (to which it had been attached since the commencement of the offensive of September 26th). The Commanding Officer, 5th Corps directed the Brigade Commander to report to the Commanding Officer, 42nd Division for instructions.

The Brigade Commander reported immediately to the Commanding Officer, 42nd Division and learned that he desired to employ the tanks the following morning between LANDRES-ET-ST. GEORGES and ST. GEORGES. Plans were rapidly made for their employment and the Commanding Officer of the Provisional Company notified while the company was still on the road to EXERMONT.

Due to the great distance of the march and the grueling speed at which tanks were forced to march in order to be in battle position at H hour, only 10 of the tanks reached the battle position. These tanks just reached their position to go over at H hour. They progressed into the enemy's trenches and there ran into what appeared to be the formation of a counterattack.

The infantry did not support the tanks, so after they had dispersed the enemy the tanks returned to EXERMONT. The 345th Battalion reached BOURG and was detached from the 304th Brigade and assigned to the 306th Brigade. The 303rd Battalion completed training on October 14th and commenced battle practice at SANDFORD and LULWORTH in ENGLAND.

DATE: October 15, 1918
AVAILABLE FOR ALL DUTY: 94 Officers and 1342 Men
WEATHER: Cloudy **LOSSES:** 1 Officer wounded; 2 Men wounded

[Notes at left margin of diary page:
"Tuesday Maps. Foret d'Argonne 1/20000.
Operating with 42nd Division."]

NARRATIVE OF OPERATIONS:

Captain Courtney Barnard in command of the Provisional Company directed by Major Brett to organize for attack on the 16th October.

Report received from Commanding Officer, Provisional Company covering tank march from VARENNES to EXERMONT, states that only 12 of the original 24 tanks arrived at the park in column, the others came on from time to time. By the time of the departure for position of departure, 17 had reported.

DATE: October 16, 1918
AVAILABLE FOR ALL DUTY: 94 Officers and 1342 Men
WEATHER: Cloudy **ROADS:** Good **HEALTH:** Good
CAMP: Good **LOSSES:** 1 Man wounded
[Notes at left margin of diary page:
"Wednesday Maps. Foret d'Argonne 1/20000.
Operating with 42nd Division."]
NARRATIVE OF OPERATIONS:
First Provisional Company still attached to 42nd Division, 5th Army Corps remained at EXERMONT.

First Lieutenant Maurice H. [Knowles], in compliance with instructions from Chief of Tank Corps and Order #1, October 11th 1st Tank Brigade, left with detachment of men, nine trucks and two Dodge cars for BOURG, 302nd Tank Center to report to the Commanding Officer thereof.

DATE: October 17, 1918
AVAILABLE FOR ALL DUTY: 94 Officers and 1342 Men
WEATHER: Cloudy **ROADS:** Good **HEALTH:** Good
CAMP: Fair
[Notes at left margin of diary page:
"Thursday Maps. Foret d'Argonne 1/20000."]
NARRATIVE OF OPERATIONS:
Ninth Company 2nd Regiment M.M.S.C.[12] ordered to move from station at CAMP FOURGOUS to VARENNES to assist 321st Repair and Salvage Company in repair and salvage.

Provisional Company remained in reserve at EXERMONT.

DATE: October 18, 1918
AVAILABLE FOR ALL DUTY: 94 Officers and 1336 Men
WEATHER: Cloudy **ROADS:** Good **HEALTH:** Good
CAMP: Fair
[Notes at left margin of diary page:
"Friday Maps. Foret d'Argonne 1/20000."]
NARRATIVE OF OPERATIONS:
Operations report of the 321st R & S Company as follows: tanks in repair park 66, on duty at EXERMONT

---

[12] Motor Mechanics Signal Corps.

31, salvaged 1, located west of AIRE RIVER 7, in river on BAULNY FLEVILLE ROAD 1, east of river 15. Total of 121 accounted for on this date, 50 in running order, remainder undergoing repairs.

The 9th M.M.S.C. arrived at VARENNES. The 1st Provisional Company remained at EXERMONT.

DATE: October 19, 1918
AVAILABLE FOR ALL DUTY: 95 Officers and 1277 Men
WEATHER: Rain **ROADS:** Good **HEALTH:** Good
CAMP: Good

[Notes at left margin of diary page:
"Saturday Maps. Foret d'Argonne 1/20000."]

NARRATIVE OF OPERATIONS:

Received memorandum from Headquarters 1st Army Corps with instructions to send special personnel requisition showing replacements needed. Eleven tanks unaccounted for, 50 in running order.

1st Provisional Company remained in EXERMONT in reserve.

DATE: October 20, 1918
AVAILABLE FOR ALL DUTY: 95 Officers and 1271 Men
WEATHER: Rain **ROADS:** Good **HEALTH:** Good
CAMP: Good

[Notes at left margin of diary page:
"Sunday Maps. Foret d'Argonne 1/20000."]

NARRATIVE OF OPERATIONS:

In compliance with memorandum Headquarters 1st Army Corps relative to replacements, the following was submitted.

Sergeants first class 2; sergeants 17, to be qualified in gas engine mechanics; corporals 27, to be qualified as tank drivers; cooks 2; privates first class 29; privates 30.

Tanks unaccounted for 8. Fifty-three tanks in running order.

No action. 1st Provisional Company remained in EXERMONT in reserve.

DATE: October 21, 1918
AVAILABLE FOR ALL DUTY: 80 Officers and 912 Men
WEATHER: Fair **ROADS:** Good **HEALTH:** Good
CAMP: Good
[Notes at left margin of diary page:
"Monday Maps. Foret d'Argonne 1/20000."]

NARRATIVE OF OPERATIONS:

Telegraphic order from General Headquarters dated October 20, 1918 revoking prior order to the effect that all officers at all times wear the insignia of rank.

Tank units of 1st Brigade allotted to the 1st Army relieved. Headquarters Company, 344th Battalion and the 1st Provisional Company to return to the 302nd Tank Center.

321st R & S Company to remain at present station.

1st Provisional Company remained at EXERMONT.

Tanks unaccounted for 8. Tanks in running order 64.

The 303rd Battalion was split up and every other man transferred to the 302nd Provisional Battalion, Tank Corps now the 306th Battalion Tank Corps.

The strength of the 303rd Battalion is now 45 Officers and 386 Men.

TELEGRAM

October 21, 1918.

Commanding General, 1st American Army.
Number 1637 G-3. The Tank Corps units allotted to 1st Army are relieved from duty therewith (period) The Commanding Officer, Headquarters 344th Battalion and the Provisional Company after returning its Tanks to Tank park at VARENNES will proceed at once to the 302nd Center, Tank Corps, for the purpose of organizing and filling up the Battalion (period) The Commanding Officer, 344th Battalion will assign a suitable officer to handle the supply and another for Adjutant and Liaison Officer to the 321st Company (period) Acknowledge.
By Order: CONNER

DATE: October 22, 1918
AVAILABLE FOR ALL DUTY: 87 Officers and 912 Men
WEATHER: Cloudy **ROADS:** Good **HEALTH:** Good
CAMP: Good

[Note at left margin of diary page:
"Map Foret d'Argonne 1/20000."]

NARRATIVE OF OPERATIONS:

A message was sent from the Commanding Officer, 1st Brigade to Chief of Tank Corps insisting that tanks were necessary for the operations contemplated in three or four days, instructions requested. The 1st Brigade had not been detached from the 1st Army Corps other than order of 1st Army of 21st but the use of tanks was contemplated under an arrangement between the Commanding Generals of the two Army Corps.

DATE: October 23, 1918
AVAILABLE FOR ALL DUTY: 91 Officers and 1002 Men
WEATHER: Cloudy **ROADS:** Good **HEALTH:** Good
CAMP: Good

NARRATIVE OF OPERATIONS:

Orders to move of the 21st revoked by V.O.C.O. 1st Army and revocation communicated to the Chief of Tank Corps at CHAUMONT.

Tank situation:

Tanks accounted for   137
Tanks unaccounted for   4
Tanks running   65
No action.

DATE: October 24, 1918
AVAILABLE FOR ALL DUTY: 90 Officers and 996 Men
WEATHER: Rain **ROADS:** Good **HEALTH:** Good
CAMP: Good

NARRATIVE OF OPERATIONS:

No Action.

1st Provisional Company at EXERMONT.

DATE: October 25, 1918
AVAILABLE FOR ALL DUTY: 89 Officers and 996 Men
WEATHER: Rain **ROADS:** Good **HEALTH:** Good
CAMP: Good

NARRATIVE OF OPERATIONS:

No Action.

1st Provisional Company at EXERMONT.

DATE: October 26, 1918
AVAILABLE FOR ALL DUTY: 89 Officers and 1002 Men
WEATHER: Cloudy **ROADS:** Good **HEALTH:** Good
CAMP: Good

NARRATIVE OF OPERATIONS:

No Action.

Twenty-five tanks left in EXERMONT for action and 10 towed to Repair and Salvage Company.

The 303rd Battalion completed battle practice at SANDFORD-LULWORTH in ENGLAND and returned to WAREHAM October 26th 1918.

———————

```
                Hqrs. 1st Brig. T.C.
                 Oct. 27, 1918
From: Commanding Officer, Advanced Detachment,
      1st Brig. T.C.
To:   Commanding Officer, 302nd Tank Center,
      A.P.O. 714
Subject: Citations.
      1. The following are officers and men on whose
acts of courage I have first-hand information.
      Captain Newell P. Weed, 344th Bn. T.C. near
the FORET D'ARGONNE, Sept. 26th, 1918. For leaving
his tank and preceding the attack on foot to
reconnoiter passage for his command, while thus
engaged he came under heavy machine gun fire and
jumped into a trench for protection only to find
himself completely surrounded by enemy. With the
assistance of a tank, which appeared, the enemy was
dispersed. Continued on foot until knocked
unconscious by a shell. Was carried to the rear, but
on regaining consciousness immediately went forward
and took command of his organization. Was almost
```

immediately gassed, but continued on duty until ordered to the rear by the battalion commander.

Captain Harry H Semmes, 344th Bn. T.C. near VAUQUOIS, France, Sept. 26, 1918. Left his tank under heavy machine gun fire and shell fire to reconnoiter a passage for his command over very difficult ground and through a heavy fog. Continued this work until wounded, thereby making it possible for his command to enter the fight at the proper time and place.

Captain Math L. English, 344th Bn. T.C. near MONTREBEAU WOODS, France on Oct. 4, 1918. Left his tank to make personal reconnaissance over difficult ground under heavy machine gun and shell fire, continued this work until killed, at which time he was 300 M. in front of Tanks and Infantry.

Corporal Harold W. Roberts, 1013943, Co. A 344th Bn. T.C. in MONTREBEAU WOODS, France, Oct. 6, 1918. When the tank he was driving fell into a water tank trap. He said to the Gunner, "Well, only one of us can get out, out you go" and with that statement shoved the Gunner through the door, and was himself drowned.

2. There are a great number of reported cases of heroism, but suggest that the citations come through the officers having accurate knowledge of the acts. I have ordered the C.O. 1st Provisional Co. and the C.O. 321st R & S Co. to make recommendations within their organizations.

SERENO E. BRETT
Major, Tank Corps

DATE: October 27, 1918
AVAILABLE FOR ALL DUTY: 94 Officers and 1015 Men
WEATHER: Cloudy **ROADS:** Good **HEALTH:** Good
CAMP: Good

NARRATIVE OF OPERATIONS:

No action.

Major Brett recommended Captains Newell P. Weed, Harry H. Semmes, Math L. English and Corporal Harold W. Roberts for recognition for extraordinary heroism in action. Letter attached.

1st Provisional Company at EXERMONT.

DATE: October 28, 1918
AVAILABLE FOR ALL DUTY: 94 Officers and 1037 Men
WEATHER: Rain **ROADS:** Good **HEALTH:** Good
CAMP: Good
NARRATIVE OF OPERATIONS:
No action.

328th still at CAMP CHAMBERLAIN performing the usual drill and camp duties.

303rd Battalion still at WAREHAM, ENGLAND performing the usual drill and camp duties.

DATE: October 29, 1918
AVAILABLE FOR ALL DUTY: 94 Officers and 1032 Men
WEATHER: Cloudy **ROADS:** Good **HEALTH:** Good
CAMP: Good **LOSSES:** 2 Men wounded
NARRATIVE OF OPERATIONS:
No action.

TELEGRAM

OCTOBER 30, 1918.

Commanding Officer, 3rd Brigade, Tank Corps, BOURG.
Commanding Officer, 302nd Tank Center BOURG.
Number 1768 G-3. The 3rd Brigade, Tank Corps, (less 306th Battalion) will proceed without delay for temporary duty with 1st Army (comma) relieving 1st Brigade, Tank Corps (period) Headquarters, 3rd Brigade and 316th Company, Tank Corps (comma) now at BOURG (comma) will move at once by own motor transportation to VARENNES (comma) reporting upon arrival to Commanding General 1st Army (period) The 345th and 331st Battalions (comma) Tank Corps (comma) now at BOURG (comma) will be sent by rail to VARENNES (comma) reporting upon arrival to Brigade Commander (period) Movement must be expedited

(period) After arrival of these units the 1st
Brigade, Tank Corps (comma) now on duty with 1st
Army (comma) will be relieved under arrangements to
be made by Commanding General, 1st Army, and Chief
of Tank Corps (period) The unit thus relieved will
be sent by rail by Commanding General, 1st Army, to
302nd Tank Center (comma) BOURG (period) Troop
Movement Bureau, these Headquarters, will arrange
for rail transportation required for above movements
(comma) and will furnish to all concerned the
necessary information regarding trains (period)
Acknowledge.

By order: CONNER

––––––––––

DATE: October 30, 1918
AVAILABLE FOR ALL DUTY: 93 Officers and 1021 Men
WEATHER: Fair **ROADS:** Good **HEALTH:** Good
CAMP: Good

NARRATIVE OF OPERATIONS:

1st Brigade relieved from duty with 1st Army and
ordered to the 302nd Tank Center. Order attached.
Tanks in order – 82.

The 303rd Battalion left WAREHAM, ENGLAND by way
of SOUTH HAMPTON to LE HAVRE.

DATE: October 31, 1918
AVAILABLE FOR ALL DUTY: 94 Officers and 1025 Men
WEATHER: Rain **ROADS:** Good **HEALTH:** Good
CAMP: Good

NARRATIVE OF OPERATIONS:

No action.

First Lieutenant Harry E. Gibbs and three men ordered
to proceed from VARENNES to BOURG, FRANCE.

PATTON WAR DIARY - NOVEMBER 1918

NOVEMBER 1918
304TH (1ST) BRIGADE
TANK CORPS.

This book is for one month;
do not tear out sheets.

WAR DIARY INSTRUCTIONS

1. Observe F. S. R., Paragraph 35.

2. This is the HISTORY of what your unit accomplishes, in other words, of OPERATIONS. Tell what actually happened; not what is supposed to have happened. Abstain from criticism.

3. Append all orders, messages, plans, sketches, etc.

4. Designate precisely each place and position occupied; assume that the reader never heard of any of them.

5. Note the personnel, losses and statistics of unit as changes occur; give dates, hours, state of weather, atmosphere and roads.

6. Enter the higher units to which you belong: brigades, divisions, corps, etc.

7. When maneuvering, always try to get the designations and positions of units next to you in line.

8. Tactical observations are particularly desired.

9. No erasures may be made in this Diary.

10. The C. O. must sign before the return is made at the end of the calendar month.

A. J. PRINTING DEPT., G. H. Q. A. E. F., 1918.

Col. 3<.

Image of cover to Patton's War Diary for November 1918.

DATE: November 1, 1918
AVAILABLE FOR ALL DUTY: 96 Officers and 1024 Men
WEATHER: Cloudy **ROADS:** Fair **HEALTH:** Good
CAMP: Good **LOSSES:** 1 Officer wounded; 1 Man wounded
CAPTURES: 4 Guns - 77's
[Note at left margin of diary page:
"Maps Argonne Montfaucon 1/50,000."]

NARRATIVE OF OPERATIONS:

Provisional Company was placed under the 2nd Division advance unit commanders; 1st Platoon under Second Lieutenant William Louisell supporting the 23rd Infantry attacked LANDRES-ET-ST.GEORGES; 2nd Platoon under Second Lieutenant Churchill C. Peters supporting the 5th Marines attacked northwest edge of LANDRES-ET-ST. GEORGES; 3rd Platoon under Second Lieutenant Floyd F. Callahan supporting 6th Marines to reduce ST. GEORGES.

Twenty-five tanks left the park at VARENNES and 20 went into action. Lieutenant Louisell was wounded early in the action. The objectives were in every case attained, the tanks being always in front of the infantry. The resistance stiffened as the attack proceeded.

———————

HEADQUARTERS
ADVANCE DETACHMENT 1st BRIGADE, TANK CORPS,
1st ARMY CORPS

S.O.)   November 2, 1918
12.)

    1. In compliance with S.O. #518, 1st Army Corps and V.O., Chief of Tank Corps, First Lieutenant Jesse L. Thompson, commanding 321st R & S Company, Tank Corps, will move his company from their present station at VARENNES and proceed to BOURG, HAUTE-MARNE, reporting upon arrival there to Commanding Officer, 1st Brigade Tank Corps.

     2. Motor transportation will be furnished as
follows: Mack 5-1/2 ton trucks, U.S. No's. 46682,
46410, 46690, 52009, 52018, 52013, 595, 52007, 5832.
Dodge automobile, U.S. no. 14700.

By order of MAJOR BRETT
H.C. BORLAND
1st Lt., T.C.
Acting Adjutant.

DATE: November 2, 1918
AVAILABLE FOR ALL DUTY: 296 Officers and 1011 Men
WEATHER: Rain **ROADS:** Fair **HEALTH:** Good
CAMP: Good
NARRATIVE OF OPERATIONS:
All available tanks were assigned to the 2nd Division for continuation of the attack and were held in reserve at LANDRES-ET-GEORGES as the 2nd Division had obtained its objective on the first day. No action.

The 321st Repair and Salvage Company moved from VARENNES to BOURG per S.O. #12 attached.

DATE: November 3, 1918
AVAILABLE FOR ALL DUTY: 92 Officers and 1023 Men
WEATHER: Cloudy **ROADS:** Good **HEALTH:** Good
CAMP: Good
NARRATIVE OF OPERATIONS:
1st Provisional Company at EXERMONT. No action.

DATE: November 4, 1918
AVAILABLE FOR ALL DUTY: 98 Officers and 1029 Men
WEATHER: Rain **ROADS:** Fair **HEALTH:** Good
CAMP: Good
NARRATIVE OF OPERATIONS:
No action.

First news of tentative Armistice terms to Germany came this afternoon. Austria has signed a separate Armistice.
1st Provisional Company in EXERMONT.

Image of "Training Schedule" found affixed adjacent to Patton's November 5 diary entry.

DATE: November 5, 1918
AVAILABLE FOR ALL DUTY: 97 Officers and 1016 Men
WEATHER: Rain **ROADS:** Fair **HEALTH:** Good
CAMP: Good

NARRATIVE OF OPERATIONS:
No Action.
Provisional Company at EXERMONT.

DATE: November 6, 1918
AVAILABLE FOR ALL DUTY: 95 Officers and 1006 Men
WEATHER: Rain **ROADS:** Fair **HEALTH:** Good
CAMP: Good

NARRATIVE OF OPERATIONS:
Provisional Company advanced to BAYONVILLE. The 3rd Brigade is in VARENNES preparing to relieve the 304th Brigade. The American troops are continuing their victorious advance.

GENERAL HEADQUARTERS, TANK CORPS,
AMERICAN EXPEDITIONARY FORCES

6 November 1918

GENERAL ORDERS :
No. 21   :
    Pursuant to designation of the War Department
the following changes in numerical designations of
Tank Corps units are announced:

    1st Prov. Brigade becomes the 304th Brigade
    2nd Prov. Brigade becomes the 305th Brigade
    3rd Prov. Brigade becomes the 306th Brigade
    4th Prov. Brigade becomes the 307th Brigade
    304th Brigade Headquarters becomes the 303rd
Tank Center, upon arrival in France.
    By command of Brigadier General Rockenbach:
        W. KRUEGER
    Lt. Col., General Staff,
        Chief of Staff

DATE: November 7, 1918
AVAILABLE FOR ALL DUTY: 96 Officers and 1063 Men
WEATHER: Rain **ROADS:** Fair **HEALTH:** Good
CAMP: Good
NARRATIVE OF OPERATIONS:
1st Provisional Company at BAYONVILLE. No action.

1st Provisional Brigade is the 304th Brigade. Copy attached.

The 303rd Brigade arrived at NEUVY-PAILLOUX INDRE, FRANCE where the regular camp and drill duties were taken up.

DATE: November 8, 1918
AVAILABLE FOR ALL DUTY: 96 Officers and 1304 Men
WEATHER: Cloudy **ROADS:** Fair **HEALTH:** Good
CAMP: Good
NARRATIVE OF OPERATIONS:
No action.

Provisional Company at BAYONVILLE.

The 344th Battalion commenced intensive training at 302nd Tank Center. A sample schedule is attached on sheet November 4th.

DATE: November 9, 1918
AVAILABLE FOR ALL DUTY: 103 Officers and 1307 Men
WEATHER: Cloudy **ROADS:** Fair **HEALTH:** Good
CAMP: Good
NARRATIVE OF OPERATIONS:
Provisional Company at BAYONVILLE.
All men of the 344th Battalion returned to VARENNES and the 307th Brigade relieved the 304th Brigade.
No action.

DATE: November 10, 1918
AVAILABLE FOR ALL DUTY: 103 Officers and 1342 Men
WEATHER: Rain **ROADS:** Fair **HEALTH:** Good
CAMP: Good
NARRATIVE OF OPERATIONS:
Major Brett and Lieutenant Borland[1] left for BOURG at 9:00 a.m. Headquarters Company left for BOURG at 12 noon.
No action.

DATE: November 11, 1918
AVAILABLE FOR ALL DUTY: 101 Officers and 1347 Men
WEATHER: Rain **ROADS:** Fair **HEALTH:** Good
CAMP: Good
NARRATIVE OF OPERATIONS:
Detachment arrived at BOURG at 8:00 p.m.
News of the signing of the Armistice arrived. Extract of G.O. #17 announces cessation of hostilities.
Strict discipline maintained.

---

[1] First Lieutenant Harry G. Borland, Tank Corps.

COMPTON WAR DIARY - AUGUST 1918

August 1918.

345 TH (321 TH) Battalion

304 TH (1st) Brigade Tank Corps

WAR DIARY INSTRUCTIONS

1. Observe F. S. R., Paragraph 35.

2. This is the HISTORY of what your unit accomplishes, in other words, of OPERATIONS. Tell what actually happened; not what is supposed to have happened. Abstain from criticism.

3. Append all orders, messages, plans, sketches, etc.

4. Designate precisely each place and position occupied; assume that the reader never heard of any of them.

5. Note the personnel, losses and statistics of unit as changes occur; give dates, hours, state of weather, atmosphere and roads.

6. Enter the higher units to which you belong: brigades, divisions, corps, etc.

7. When maneuvering, always try to get the designations and positions of units next to you in line.

8. Tactical observations are particularly desired.

9. No erasures may be made in this Diary.

10. The C. O. must sign before the return is made at the end of the calendar month.

Laurel Compton

A. G. Printing Dept., G. H. Q., A. E. F., 1918.

Capt. Paul Compton.

Comdg 345th Bn.

Image of cover to Compton's War Diary for August 1918.

HEADQUARTERS, 345th BATTALION, 306th BRIGADE,
TANK CORPS.

24th January 1919
From: Commanding Officer, 345th Battalion
To: Colonel G.S. Patton, Jr., 304th Brigade,
           Tank Corps.
Subject: War Diary.

I hand you herewith war diary covering the period of
21st August to 31st October 1918, also two field message
books[1] containing copies of messages sent and messages,
orders and memorandums covering the dates 26th September
to 11th October 1918.

                    RANULF COMPTON
                    Captain, Tank Corps.

DATE: August 21, 1918
ORGANIZATION: 345th Battalion at Varennes Marne,
France
AVAILABLE FOR ALL DUTY: 24 Officers and 301 Men
WEATHER: Fair **HEALTH:** Good **CAMP:** Good
NARRATIVE OF OPERATIONS:

In accordance with G.O. 114 [or 115—last digit unclear],
Headquarters First Tank Center, 19th August 1918,
Captain Ranulf Compton took command of the 345th
Battalion, then the 327th Battalion, Tank Corps, at 6:00
a.m., 21st August 1918, at BRENNES, FRANCE, where it
was then stationed.

By V.O.C.O. Captain Compton was ordered to get the
battalion ready to leave for the front at once. With that in
view we had a review course in firing both the 37mm and
machine guns from the tanks, as well as company schools
conducted by the company commanders which continued
from 22nd August 1918 to 6th September 1918.

---

[1] The two field message books were not found with the archived war
diary collection.

DATE: August 22, 1918
AVAILABLE FOR ALL DUTY: 24 Officers and 299 Men
WEATHER: Fair **HEALTH:** Good **CAMP:** Good
NARRATIVE OF OPERATIONS:
Battalion instruction and company schools continued.

DATE: August 23, 1918
AVAILABLE FOR ALL DUTY: 19 Officers and 281 Men
WEATHER: Fair **HEALTH:** Good **CAMP:** Good
NARRATIVE OF OPERATIONS:
Battalion instruction and company schools continued.

DATE: August 24, 1918
AVAILABLE FOR ALL DUTY: 19 Officers and 281 Men
WEATHER: Cloudy **HEALTH:** Good **CAMP:** Good
NARRATIVE OF OPERATIONS:
General policing and battalion inspection. Inspecting Officer, Captain Ranulf Compton.

DATE: August 25, 1918
AVAILABLE FOR ALL DUTY: 17 Officers and 241 Men
HEALTH: Good **CAMP:** Good
NARRATIVE OF OPERATIONS:
No work or instruction. Reveille and taps. Roll call.

DATE: August 26, 1918
AVAILABLE FOR ALL DUTY: 20 Officers and 239 Men
HEALTH: Good **CAMP:** Good
NARRATIVE OF OPERATIONS:
Battalion instruction and company schools and drills.

DATE: August 27, 1918
AVAILABLE FOR ALL DUTY: 21 Officers and 242 Men
HEALTH: Good **CAMP:** Good
NARRATIVE OF OPERATIONS:
Received 36 Renault Light Tanks from the Berlier factory at Cercottes, France.
To "A" Company were issued 24 tanks, "B" Company 12. Drills and instruction continued.

DATE: August 28, 1918
AVAILABLE FOR ALL DUTY: 23 Officers and 300 Men
HEALTH: Good **CAMP:** Good
NARRATIVE OF OPERATIONS:
Received 30 Renault Light Tanks from the Berlier factory at Cercottes, France.

To "B" Company were issued 12, "C" Company 18.

Drills and instruction continued.

DATE: August 29, 1918
AVAILABLE FOR ALL DUTY: 23 Officers and 288 Men
HEALTH: Good **CAMP:** Good
NARRATIVE OF OPERATIONS:
Ordnance equipment – 37mm guns and machine gun in all tanks were given a field test.

Ammunition to fill all tanks was issued and installed.

DATE: August 30, 1918
AVAILABLE FOR ALL DUTY: 23 Officers and 289 Men
WEATHER: Cloudy **HEALTH:** Good **CAMP:** Good
NARRATIVE OF OPERATIONS:
All tank crews had tank drill and firing instruction on rifle range.

DATE: August 31, 1918
AVAILABLE FOR ALL DUTY: 23 Officers and 294 Men
NARRATIVE OF OPERATIONS:
General policing and inspection.

COMPTON WAR DIARY - SEPTEMBER 1918

September 1918.

345TH (327TH) Battalion

304TH (14) Brigade

Tank Corps

WAR DIARY INSTRUCTIONS

1. Observe F. S. R., Paragraph 35.

2. This is the HISTORY of what your unit accomplishes, in other words, of OPERATIONS. Tell what actually happened; not what is supposed to have happened. Abstain from criticism.

3. Append all orders, messages, plans, sketches, etc.

4. Designate precisely each place and position occupied; assume that the reader never heard of any of them.

5. Note the personnel, losses and statistics of unit as changes occur; give dates, hours, state of weather, atmosphere and roads.

6. Enter the higher units to which you belong: brigades, divisions, corps, etc.

7. When maneuvering, always try to get the designations and positions of units next to you in line.

8. Tactical observations are particularly desired.

9. No erasures may be made in this Diary.

10. The C. O. must sign before the return is made at the end of the calendar month.

Ranulf Compton

A. & PRINTING DEPT., G. H. Q. A. E. F., 1918.

Capt. Tank Corps.

Comdg 345th Bn.

Image of cover to Compton's War Diary for September 1918.

DATE: September 1, 1918
AVAILABLE FOR ALL DUTY: 24 Officers and 300 Men
WEATHER: Fair **ROADS:** Good **HEALTH:** Good
CAMP: Good

[Notes at left margin of diary page:
"Sunday. Map Vigneulles-A 1/30,000."]

NARRATIVE OF OPERATIONS:

The Battalion Commander, Captain Ranulf Compton accompanied by his Company Commanders Captains Gilfillan, Williams and Barnard of "A," "B," and "C" Companies respectively went to the vicinity of HAUDIMONT (341.3-260-6)[1] where they made their personal initial reconnaissance in company with the brigade and battalion reconnaissance officers who had been preparing the problem for some time, for a proposed attack from the west side of the ST. MIHIEL SALIENT.

Companies continued drill and instruction.

DATE: September 2, 1918
ORGANIZATION: 327th Battalion **FROM:** Brennes Ville
HOUR: 8:00 a.m. **TO:** Brennes Railroad Station
DISTANCE: 1.5 kilometers
AVAILABLE FOR ALL DUTY: 24 Officers and 296 Men
WEATHER: Cloudy **ROADS:** Good **HEALTH:** Good
CAMP: Good

NARRATIVE OF OPERATIONS:

In accordance with V.O.C.O. the battalion left the village of BRENNES and went into camp in shelter tents near the railroad station of BRENNES where the tanks and all transportation, material, etc., were concentrated.

DATE: September 3, 1918
AVAILABLE FOR ALL DUTY: 25 Officers and 308 Men
WEATHER: Fair **ROADS:** Good **HEALTH:** Good
CAMP: Good

NARRATIVE OF OPERATIONS:

Received 6 tanks, the balance of the tanks allotted to the battalion being 72 in all, from Berlier factory at

---

[1] Spelled "Haudiomont" in Brigade War Diary for September 1.

CERCOTTES, FRANCE. These were issued to Company "C" and the guns given a field test.

DATE: September 4, 1918
AVAILABLE FOR ALL DUTY: 25 Officers and 315 Men
WEATHER: Fair **ROADS:** Good **HEALTH:** Good
CAMP: Good
NARRATIVE OF OPERATIONS:
Drill, instruction and fatigue.

DATE: September 5, 1918
AVAILABLE FOR ALL DUTY: 25 Officers and 315 Men
WEATHER: Fair **ROADS:** Good **HEALTH:** Good
CAMP: Good
NARRATIVE OF OPERATIONS:
Drill, instruction and fatigue.

DATE: September 6, 1918
AVAILABLE FOR ALL DUTY: 25 Officers and 315 Men
WEATHER: Rain **ROADS:** Fair **HEALTH:** Good
CAMP: Good
NARRATIVE OF OPERATIONS:
Drill, instruction and fatigue.

DATE: September 7, 1918
AVAILABLE FOR ALL DUTY: 26 Officers and 317 Men
WEATHER: Rainy **ROADS:** Fair **HEALTH:** Good
CAMP: Good
[Notes at left margin of diary page:
"Saturday. Map Mort Mare 1/20." However, Map Mort Mare referenced in Patton's diary for September indicates a scale of 1/20,000.]
NARRATIVE OF OPERATIONS:
Battalion assigned to the 1st Brigade, Tank Corps Lieutenant Colonel G. S. Patton, Commanding by General Order No. 13, General Headquarters, Tank Corps, 20 August 1918.

Battalion Commander, Captain Ranulf Compton went by automobile to BERNECOURT and established Battalion Command Post. First section of the battalion, "A" Company and one-half of "B" Company entrained to move to the BOIS DE LA HAZELLE (359.8-31.7) near BERNECOURT (361.0-29.9).

DATE: September 8, 1918
AVAILABLE FOR ALL DUTY: 27 Officers and 327 Men
WEATHER: Rain **HEALTH:** Good **CAMP:** Good
[Notes at left margin of diary page: "Sunday. Map Mort Mare 1/20."]
NARRATIVE OF OPERATIONS:
The balance of the battalion, one-half of "B" Company and "C" Company entrained to move to the BOIS DE LA HAZELLE near BERNECOURT.
Battalion Command Post, BERNECOURT (361.0-29.9).

DATE: September 9, 1918
AVAILABLE FOR ALL DUTY: 27 Officers and 327 Men
WEATHER: Cloudy **HEALTH:** Good **CAMP:** Good
[Notes at left margin of diary page: "Monday. Map Mort Mare 1/20."]
NARRATIVE OF OPERATIONS:
Battalion en route.
Battalion Command Post, BERNECOURT (361.29.9).

DATE: September 10, 1918
ORGANIZATION: Company "A," 327th Battalion
FROM: 362.5-28.5 **HOUR:** 10:00 p.m. **TO:** Bois de la Hazelle **HOUR:** 1:30 a.m. **DISTANCE:** 5 kilometers
ORGANIZATION: One-half Company "B," 327th Battalion
FROM: 362.5-28.5 **HOUR:** 10:30 p.m. **TO:** Bois de la Hazelle **HOUR:** 2:00 a.m. **DISTANCE:** 5 kilometers
AVAILABLE FOR ALL DUTY: 27 Officers and 327 Men
WEATHER: Rainy **ROADS:** Poor **HEALTH:** Good
CAMP: Fair
NARRATIVE OF OPERATIONS:
First section train carrying "A" Company and one-half of "B" Company reached a point 362.5-28.5 north of the BOIS DE REHANNE about 8:00 p.m. They proceeded to unload and marched to the BOIS DE LA HAZELLE (359.8-31.7), a

distance of 5 kilometers. All tanks arrived and made camp by 3:00 a.m.

Map Mort Mare 1/20.

DATE: September 11, 1918
AVAILABLE FOR ALL DUTY: 27 Officers and 327 men
WEATHER: Rainy **ROADS:** Poor **HEALTH:** Good
CAMP: Fair

NARRATIVE OF OPERATIONS:

Effort to locate second section of train or tank officer in charge of the routing and placing of the train was unsuccessful, although the Battalion Commander, Captain Ranulf Compton and the battalion staff sought them throughout the whole day.

DATE: September 12, 1918
ORGANIZATION: Companies "A" and "B," 345th Battalion
FROM: Bois de la Hazelle **HOUR:** 10:00 on the 11th
TO: Bois du Jury **HOUR:** 1:00 a.m.
DISTANCE: 1.5 kilometer
ORGANIZATION: 345th Battalion
FROM: Jump off at 5:30 a.m. **TO:** Bois de Beney
DISTANCE: 15 kilometers
AVAILABLE FOR ALL DUTY: 27 Officers and 327 Men
WEATHER: Rainy **ROADS:** Poor **HEALTH:** Good
CAMP: Fair **LOSSES:** 1 Officer wounded; 2 Men killed
CAPTURES: 75 Men and 10 guns est. [sic]

[Notes at left margin of diary page:
"Thursday. Map Mort Mare 1/20. Attack with 42nd Division,
89th Division on right; 1st Division on left,
4th Corps 1st Army. Map Foret Argonne 1/20 [sic]
Attached by S.O. 120, 1st Army,
3 Sept. 1918; S.O. 135, 1st Army,
5 Sept. 1918. (360.0-34.4) (358.9-35.0)."]

NARRATIVE OF OPERATIONS:

General Order No. 16, General Headquarters Tank Corps, 12th September 1918 changed 327th Battalion to 345th Battalion. The battalion second section train arrived about 1:00 a.m. at the north edge of BOIS DE

GROSROUVRE (361.2-26.5). They marched to BOIS DU
JURY (359.1-32.4) about 9 kilometers.

The first tank arrived about 6:45 a.m. "A" and "B"
Companies were in position at the designated point of
departure (358.85-32.6) at 1:00 a.m. At 5:00 a.m., the
official "H" hour, the tanks took off with the infantry.

At 9:00 a.m. the Battalion Commander reported:

    25 tanks engaged
    11 tanks disabled in action
    10 disabled at or near P.D.[2]
     3 going into action
    _7 supply tanks
    56 total
    16 brigade reserve
    72 total battalion tanks

Most of the tanks disabled at the point of departure
were tanks of Company "C" which was late in arriving owing
to the delay on the railroad. Small repairs and regassing
put seven in commission and they went with the Battalion
Commander into action as a battle reserve.

The battalion was directed to attack between the eastern
edge of BOIS DE REMIERES (359.0-33.7) and the western
edge of BOIS DE LA SONNARD in the direction of ESSEY
(359.0-38.3) with two companies in the front echelon, each
company having two platoons in the front line and one in
support; the third company in each battalion forming the
battalion reserve.

The tanks of the battalion rendered assistance to the
infantry in its advance, particularly Captain Gilfillan,
Company "A" and one of his platoons who attacked the
southern edge of the BOIS DE LA SONNARD (359.0-34.?),[3]
putting out machine gun nests there.

The going was extremely heavy owing to the difficult
terrain which was made almost impassible by the five-day
rain preceding the attack. While crossing the TRENCH DES

---

[2] Point of Departure.
[3] Last digit blurred out.

HOUBLONS (358.5-35.3) the tanks came under heavy shell fire and two tanks were put out of action by direct hits.

One platoon of tanks with the infantry took the town of ESSEY (359.0-38.3) and again at the town of PANNES (358.6-39.0). The tanks rendered excellent service in reducing the resistance from the town and aiding the infantry to take many prisoners.

Lieutenant Knowles[4] of the brigade staff who commandeered a tank, and Corporal Pattison in another tank, both took 20 or more prisoners each in attacking the town of ESSEY.

First Lieutenant Tom W. Saul as technical officer in the battalion should be specially mentioned for his services. As the terrain was very difficult, breakdowns and ditching of the tanks were numerous. Lieutenant Saul not only gave his attention to his own duties, but directed the engineer officers who were present to make lanes for the tanks across the trenches and after selecting the routes and having the lanes made he personally led the tanks through the maze of the trenches and thus greatly expedited the advance of the tanks.

The battalion reserve owing to its fresh supply of gas and by taking full advantage of the tank lanes already made was able to pass to the town of PANNES where most of the tanks were obliged to stop for a refill of gas which had not yet arrived.

The battalion reserve under Captain Ranulf Compton with five tanks went on to the town of BENEY (360.4-242.0) (Map Chambley 1/20), with a platoon from the U.S. 167th Infantry. They occupied the town and took at least one 77 and five long 150's. Only a few scattering Boche were seen and the party of infantry and tanks continued on to the BOIS DE BENEY and then fell back to the main body of the 167th Infantry, who dug in just to the south of the town of BENEY (359.5-241.0) and there spent the night.

---

[4] First Lieutenant Maurice H. Knowles, Tank Corps.

Tanks of the battalion had reached a point about 15 kilometers from the point of departure. They had been of material assistance to the infantry in capturing great quantities of machine guns, field pieces of large and small caliber and immense quantities of stores and supplies in the several towns. The Boche located the infantry line and one tank which became disabled in a field to the south of BENEY and shelled these objectives intermittently through the night.

The battalion reserve remained under cover near the lines without any casualties to either tanks or personnel. Captain Gilfillan joined the reserve just at dusk. Lieutenant Isom, M.C.[5] set up his first aid station in the French front line trenches and did excellent service.

DATE: September 13, 1918
AVAILABLE FOR ALL DUTY: 27 Officers and 327 Men
WEATHER: Rain a.m. Fair p.m. **ROADS:** Poor
HEALTH: Good **CAMP:** Fair
[Notes at left margin of diary page:
"Friday. Map Chambley 1/20, Map Mort Mare 1/20."]
NARRATIVE OF OPERATIONS:

At 5:00 a.m. Captain Ranulf Compton set up the 345th Battalion Command Post in the town of PANNES (358.1-39.0). At 6:30 a.m. one company of tanks (15) which included the tanks of the three Company Commanders, Captain Gilfillan, Captain Williams and Captain Barnard of "A," "B" and "C" Companies respectively, reported to General MacArthur, 84th Infantry Brigade Commander at a point 356.5-246.8 west and north of ST. BENOIT (357.3-244.6).

As his brigade had accomplished its mission, or at least was not to attack that day, he sent them some distance to the rear where he could readily call for them should they be needed and they camouflaged at BOIS DE BENEY (358.1-243.0), as instructed.

---

[5] First Lieutenant Alphonse Isom, Medical Corps.

80

By noon Captain Compton had dispatched 20 tanks to the same place in addition to those already at the front, making 35 tanks held in reserve by the infantry brigade commander.

At 8:00 p.m. under V.O.C.O. the tanks moved from BOIS DE BENEY (358.1-243.0) to the edge of BOIS DE THIAUCOURT (358.5-40.7).

At 10:00 a.m. Lieutenant Struyk,[6] 345th Battalion Supply Officer had reported to Captain Compton with four trucks containing rations, gas, oil and ammunition. By orders of Lieutenant Colonel Patton, Tank Brigade Commander, these supplies were divided with the 344th Battalion (formerly the 326th Battalion) who were without these necessities and the necessary two trucks reported to Major Sereno E. Brett, Commanding 344th Battalion at VIGNEULLES (351.3-244.?).[7]

At 11:55 p.m. Captain Compton received a message from the Commanding Officer, Lieutenant Colonel Patton, to "go to the assistance of the infantry against a Boche counterattack." The battalion was ready and stood by until daylight, but the expected attack did not take place. Lieutenant Isom, M.C., had followed the tanks and set up his dressings station in PANNES near the Battalion Command Post.

DATE: September 14, 1918
AVAILABLE FOR ALL DUTY: 27 Officers and 327 Men
WEATHER: Rain **ROADS:** Poor **HEALTH:** Good
CAMP: Fair
> [Notes at left margin of diary page:
> "Saturday. Map Mort Mare 1/20."]
NARRATIVE OF OPERATIONS:
The battalion made minor repairs and tuned up the tanks for a move which was to take place. The Headquarters, 1st Brigade Tanks order came late in the afternoon and the movement to the former point of

---

[6] First Lieutenant Gus Struyk, Tank Corps.

[7] Last digit unclear, but appears to be either a 3 or a 5.

assembly at BOIS DE LA HAZELLE (359.8-31.7) began at 7:00 that night. With few exceptions the tanks of the battalion reached their destination and had made camp by 1:00 the following morning.

DATE: September 15, 1918
AVAILABLE FOR ALL DUTY: 26 Officers and 321 Men
WEATHER: Fair **ROADS:** Fair **HEALTH:** Good **CAMP:** Fair
[Notes at left margin of diary page:
"Sunday. Map Mort Mare 1/20."]
NARRATIVE OF OPERATIONS:
The 345th Battalion Command Post was moved to BERNECOURT (361.0-29.9) not far from the BOIS DE LA HAZELLE (359.8-31.7).

The companies began to reorganize by bringing in their disabled tanks and collecting their personnel which had gone with the infantry as per orders as soon as their tanks had become disabled in action; and were in consequence somewhat scattered.

DATE: September 16, 1918
AVAILABLE FOR ALL DUTY: 26 Officers and 321 Men
WEATHER: Fair **ROADS:** Fair **HEALTH:** Good **CAMP:** Fair
[Notes at left margin of diary page:
"Monday. Map Mort Mare 1/20."]
NARRATIVE OF OPERATIONS:
Reorganizing and making repairs of all kinds to the tanks.

Camp and command post remain at the same place.

DATE: September 17, 1918
AVAILABLE FOR ALL DUTY: 26 Officers and 321 Men
WEATHER: Rain **ROADS:** Fair **HEALTH:** Good **CAMP:** Fair
[Notes at left margin of diary page:
"Tuesday. Map Mort Mare 1/20."]
NARRATIVE OF OPERATIONS:
Reorganizing and making repairs of all kinds to the tanks.

Camp and command post remain at the same place.

DATE: September 18, 1918
AVAILABLE FOR ALL DUTY: 26 Officers and 316 Men
WEATHER: Raining **ROADS:** Fair **HEALTH:** Good
CAMP: Fair

[Notes at left margin of diary page:
"Wednesday. Map Mort Mare 1/20."]

NARRATIVE OF OPERATIONS:

A report of operations as well as a complete report of the status of the battalion personnel was submitted through channels to the Chief of Tank Corps.

In accordance with instructions ten tanks were dispatched under Lieutenants Higgins and Llewellyn on detached service as per orders Commanding Officer, 302nd Center Tank Corps.

The tanks were loaded on trucks first in order to move to their destination but this was not found practical and they were held until the following day. They were then loaded on flat cars on the DECAUVILLE RAILROAD operated by the French Army and proceeded as ordered.

DATE: September 19, 1918
AVAILABLE FOR ALL DUTY: 26 Officers and 316 Men
WEATHER: Rain **ROADS:** Fair **HEALTH:** Good
CAMP: Good

[Notes at left margin of diary page:
"Thursday. Map Mort Mare 1/20."]

NARRATIVE OF OPERATIONS:

Captain Ranulf Compton reported to 4th Corps Headquarters and received road orders for the movement into another sector.

Battalion had light duty and finished repair work on tanks.

DATE: September 20, 1918
AVAILABLE FOR ALL DUTY: 27 Officers and 326 Men
WEATHER: Cloudy **ROADS:** Fair **HEALTH:** Good
CAMP: Fair

[Notes at left margin of diary page:
"Friday. Map Mort Mare 1/20."]

NARRATIVE OF OPERATIONS:

At 1:00, 2:00 and 3:00 p.m., "C," "B," and "A" Companies respectively left their rendezvous and proceeded to the entraining point 362.8-28.4, two kilometers south of BERNECOURT, all there by 4:00 in the afternoon. The tanks remained there during the night awaiting the rail transportation.

DATE: September 21, 1918
AVAILABLE FOR ALL DUTY: 26 Officers and 317 Men
WEATHER: Rain **ROADS:** Fair **HEALTH:** Good
CAMP: Good

NARRATIVE OF OPERATIONS:

At 9:30, the first section began to load and left at about noon. The second section left about 6:00 the same night.

The Battalion Command Post was moved by truck and automobile to a woods about one kilometer north of CLERMONT-EN-ARGONNE, which was also to be the P. of A.[8]

DATE: September 22, 1918
AVAILABLE FOR ALL DUTY: 26 Officers and 317 Men
WEATHER: Cloudy **ROADS:** Good **HEALTH:** Good
CAMP: Good

NARRATIVE OF OPERATIONS:

The Battalion Command Post was moved to a point near the railroad station in CLERMONT. This move was made necessary by the fact that the Boche had discovered tanks in the woods near the former command post, and they shelled the place very heavily.

The last named point of assembly had several advantages. It was comparatively safe from shell fire since it

---

[8] Point of Assembly.

was on the reverse slope of a steep hill, offered excellent barracks for the men and was near the point of detraining when the battalion tanks would arrive.

DATE: September 23, 1918
AVAILABLE FOR ALL DUTY: 28 Officers and 330 Men
WEATHER: Rain **ROADS:** Poor **HEALTH:** Good
CAMP: Good
NARRATIVE OF OPERATIONS:
The battalion remained on their trains enroute on the 23rd September. Owing partly to the fact that the enemy shells had broken the rail line in several places, a circuitous route was made necessary to reach CLERMONT.

DATE: September 24, 1918
AVAILABLE FOR ALL DUTY: 26 Officers and 315 men
WEATHER: Rain **ROADS:** Poor **HEALTH:** Good
CAMP: Good
NARRATIVE OF OPERATIONS:
Two trains containing all of the 345th Battalion tanks not on detached service, 56 in all, and three tanks belonging to the 344th Battalion arrived and were unloaded and concealed in the woods near detraining point on reverse slope of the hill before 10:00 in the morning.

DATE: September 25, 1918
ORGANIZATION: 345th Battalion, "B" and "C" Companies
FROM: Point of Departure **HOUR:** 7:00 p.m. **TO:** Point of Assembly **HOUR:** 11:00 p.m. **DISTANCE:** 8 kilometers
ORGANIZATION: 345th Battalion, "A" Company
FROM: Point of Departure **HOUR:** 7:00 p.m. **TO:** Point of Assembly **HOUR:** 11:00 p.m. **DISTANCE:** 8 kilometers
AVAILABLE FOR ALL DUTY: 27 Officers and 313 Men
WEATHER: Cloudy **ROADS:** Good **HEALTH:** Good
CAMP: Good
[Notes at left margin of diary page:
"Wednesday. Foret D'Argonne 1/20, Verdun A 1/20."
Note that Field Order No. 2, dated September 25, 1918,
found in brigade war diary cites
Verdun A Foret D'Argonne Map at 1/20000.]

NARRATIVE OF OPERATIONS:

The company officers and certain non-commissioned officers made the reconnaissance of the sector with the Battalion Reconnaissance Officer Lieutenant Bolan. The Battalion Commander attempted to establish liaison with the various commands pertaining to his battalion in the attack.

At 7:00 p.m., the battalion left the point of assembly. Companies "B" and "C" arrived at their position in readiness east of AIRE RIVER (04.2-68.0) about 11:00 p.m. with 39 tanks—32 combat, 7 reserve and supply. Three tanks requiring major repairs did not come up.

Company "A" arrived at position in reserve, west of AIRE RIVER (03.2-67.8) about 10:00 p.m., with its full quota of 20 tanks—16 combat and 4 reserve and supply.

The 4th French Army on the west of the ARGONNE FOREST began their artillery preparation at 11:00 p.m.

Temporary command post of Captain Compton Commanding 345th Battalion dug out in LES COTES DE FORIMONT (05.3-67.55).

DATE: September 26, 1918
ORGANIZATION: 345th Battalion, "B" and "C" Companies
FROM: Cote Forimont [sic] **HOUR:** 5:30 a.m. **TO:** Cheppy
HOUR: 9:30 a.m. **DISTANCE:** 6.5 kilometers
ORGANIZATION: 345th Battalion, "A" Company
FROM: Abancourt Ferme **HOUR:** 5:30 a.m. **TO:** Varennes
HOUR: 10:00 a.m. **DISTANCE:** 7 kilometers
AVAILABLE FOR ALL DUTY: 27 Officers and 311 Men
WEATHER: Fog a.m.–Fair **ROADS:** Poor **HEALTH:** Good
CAMP: Good **LOSSES:** 1 Officer killed and I Officer wounded
[Notes at left margin of diary page:
"Thursday. Map Foret D'Argonne Verdun A 1/20.
Operating with 38th Division on Right,
28th Division on Left, 5th Corps, 1st Army."]

NARRATIVE OF OPERATIONS:

At 1:00 a.m. Americans began their artillery preparation. At 5:30 a.m. ("H" hour) the battalion (less

Company "A"), which was to be held in reserve until the following day, moved off with the 35th Division, Captain Compton and Lieutenant Bolan leading, in time to follow the 137th and 138th U.S. Infantry, who were the assaulting regiments.

There was a very dense fog and the lines moved slowly. The 345th Battalion tanks moved up and arrived at a hill just north of OUVRIER ADEN (04.6-72.4) and just south of the town of CHEPPY (05.2-73.8) at about 9:15 a.m.

About this time the fog lifted and the enemy shelled the tanks with 150's and other calibre guns, and then began a very disagreeable machine gun barrage directed at the personnel of the French Groups of Tanks who were endeavoring to cross the TRENCHES DES EUNUQUES (04.7-72.5) at this point and at the 345th Battalion personnel.

The few scattered infantrymen on the hill mentioned above fell back. The Tank Brigade Commander, Lieutenant Colonel Patton, who was present at this time, ordered the 345th Battalion into action against the hill.

Two French Schneider Tanks were disabled in the lane across the trenches but the tanks of the 345th Battalion found crossing elsewhere and proceeded to go over the hill.

With their platoons, Lieutenants Phillips and Cleworth[9] went around the west edge of the hill, while Lieutenant Mitchell[10] took his platoon over the crest, with their Company Commander Captain Williams, Company "B," following Lieutenants Nelms, Younglove[11] and Gleason in the order named from left to right, crossed over and around the eastern part of the hill, Captain Barnard, Company "C," Commanding.

The Battalion Commander crossed over the crest of the hill and then joined Lieutenant Phillips' platoon which was

---

[9] Second Lieutenant Clarence W. Cleworth, Tank Corps.
[10] Second Lieutenant Edward J. Mitchell.
[11] Second Lieutenant Joseph R. Younglove.

engaged in taking the trenches to the west of the hill and south of the town of CHEPPY.

A major of infantry assembled about 100 men at this place and with the tanks in advance flanked CHEPPY by covering the terrain towards the west and north. After passing over the trenches, the infantry took some prisoners.

This detachment was subject to a heavy fire from an enemy field piece from the rear and toward VARENNES (03.5-73.4). Captain Barnard was ordered to send a platoon to put the gun out. Firing from the tanks with the infantry, however, silenced the piece and Captain Barnard, who accompanied the platoon and had followed the CHEPPY-VARENNES highway, was not able to find it and returned within the hour.

Meantime the other tanks of the battalion had come to the assistance of the 138th Infantry in front of CHEPPY and the town was cleaned out. The infantry losses had been very heavy up to this time both from shell fire and machine guns. The machine gun fire was silenced, but the shell fire continued. There was no counter artillery fire apparently and the Boche plane flew over constantly until the middle of the afternoon, observing and directing artillery fire.

Lieutenant Colonel Patton had been wounded directly after the 345th Battalion was ordered into the attack. Captain Compton, by verbal orders of Lieutenant Colonel Patton, was placed in command of all advance tanks until relieved by Major Brett, who commanded the 344th Battalion.

At about 3:00 the tanks in the 345th Battalion were ordered to reorganize at a point south of the town of CHEPPY. At about 3:30 p.m., Lieutenant Buckley, Company "A," 344th Battalion reported to Captain Compton with nine tanks ready for duty.[12]

He reported that the Company Commander, Captain Semmes, had been seriously wounded while the company was attempting to pass to the east around

---

[12] First Lieutenant Leslie H. Buckley.

VAUQUOIS (06.0-70.9) and not finding it possible to do so, the captain had ordered the lieutenant to take command and to return to the south of VAUQUOIS and proceed along the axis of liaison and report as soon as possible to the front for action.

Captain English, Company "C," 344th Battalion also reported about this time with two tanks. The French Groups Tanks, 14 and 17, were reorganizing at the foot of the hill south of CHEPPY.

Major General Traub[13] commanding the 35th Division rode up and established a command post in a shell hole, as did Captain Compton nearby. As Major Brett had not appeared to take command, Captain Compton reported to the general as commanding the brigade of tanks.

The general, after viewing the situation and receiving a verbal report of the action from Captain Compton, ordered the latter to send one company of tanks, preferably the remainder of French Groups, towards VERY (06.0-75.8) to assist the infantry and the several French tanks which were operating in that direction.

The French tanks were not able to leave at once, and Captain Compton ordered Lieutenant Buckley to report with his nine tanks and ordered the two tanks of Company "C," 344th Battalion to join Lieutenant Buckley, making eleven tanks in all. This gave Captain English an opportunity to find and reorganize his company.

Lieutenant Buckley went at once to VERY and was able to give valuable assistance in the subsequent attack which took the town. He assembled near VERY as he was ordered, and spent the night there. Captain English also arrived at VERY with his company during the night. The remaining tanks were ordered held for further orders the next morning and were camouflaged in the woods at OUVRIER ADEN (04.6-72.4).

Company "A," 345th Battalion, Captain Gilfillan, Commanding, with the 28th Division went into action at

---

[13] Major General Peter E. Traub.

PTE. BOUREUILLES (03.5-70.9) on the west bank of the AIRE RIVER, where they were following Company "B," 344th Battalion, as a reserve company.

The two companies took the town and preceding the infantry went into VARENNES (03.5-73.4). Here the resistance was so strong that the infantry could not follow. Captain Gilfillan was seriously wounded and his tank totally disabled by an enemy shell.

The tanks fell back to the infantry and Lieutenant Mayne[14] and his platoon of Company "A," 345th Battalion was subsequently followed by a party of infantry and under a severe fire from anti-tank guns, shells and machine guns took the town the second time and the infantry occupied it.

After exploiting the terrain in front of the town, Lieutenant Brown, to whom fell the command of "A" Company, 345th Battalion, assembled the company at PTE. BOUREUILLES where Company "A," 344th Battalion had also assembled. They spent the night there.

Lieutenant Chamberlain[15] was killed at VARENNES.

DATE: September 27, 1918
ORGANIZATION: 344th Battalion, Companies "A" and "C"
FROM: Very **TO:** Point northwest **DISTANCE:** 1 kilometer
ORGANIZATION: 345th Battalion, Companies "B" and "C"
FROM: Cheppy **TO:** Baulny **DISTANCE:** 4 kilometers
ORGANIZATION: 344th Battalion, Company "B" and 345th Battalion, Company "A" **FROM:** Varennes
TO: Montblainville **DISTANCE:** 3 kilometers
AVAILABLE FOR ALL DUTY: 25 Officers and 314 Men
WEATHER: Rain **ROADS:** Poor **HEALTH:** Good
CAMP: Poor **LOSSES:** 1 Officer wounded; 1 Man killed and 1 Man wounded

---

[14] Second Lieutenant Harry M. Mayne.

[15] While listed in the Tank Corps roster as Second Lieutenant Guy R. Chamberlain, he is buried in Arlington Cemetery as Guy R. Chamberlin. http://www.arlingtoncemetery.net/grchamberlin.htm

[Notes at left margin of diary page:
"Friday. Map Foret D'Argonne Verdun A 1/20.
Operating with 38th Division on Right,
28th Division on Left, 5th Corps, 1st Army."]

NARRATIVE OF OPERATIONS:

Written orders from Major Brett, Acting Commander of the 1st Tank Brigade with the 1st Army Corps Headquarters at LES COTES DE FORIMONT (05.5-67.7) by direction of the General, placed Captain Compton in command of "all tanks on the front," which included the 14th and 17th French Tank Groups, Major Chanoine, Commanding, and the 344th and 345th Battalions, Tank Corps.

By orders of Captain Compton, the four companies, namely, Companies "A" and "C," 344th Battalion and Companies "B" and "C," 345th Battalion, were placed under command of Captain Barnard, operating in the sector on the east bank of the AIRE RIVER.

Lieutenant Brown was placed in command of the two companies, namely, Company "B," 344th Battalion and Company "A," 345th Battalion, operating in the sector on the west bank of the AIRE RIVER. Major Chanoine with his two French Groups, 14th and 17th, continued to operate in the east sector.

Captain Compton established his command post with the 28th Division at Varennes (03.5-73.4) and liaison was established forward with the Tank Groups and to the rear with Major Brett by means of runners, until such time as telephone lines could be laid or become available.

Communication with the 35th Division was maintained by telephone.

The tanks operated in three groups during the day. On the right Lieutenant Grant in command of "A" Company, 344th Battalion, moved out from VERY with the infantry and Captain English, Company "C," 344th Battalion, who was reorganizing, was held in reserve. Only small gains were made and the infantry consolidated their lines.

In the center, Captain Williams, Company "B," 345th Battalion, moved toward CHARPENTRY (03.2-76.7) from the west, with Captain Barnard, Company "C," 345th Battalion in reserve; with the French Groups attacking CHARPENTRY from the south, the town was occupied but not consolidated, and the infantry dug in outside the town.

On the west, Lieutenant Brown with Company "B," 344th Battalion and Company "A," 345th Battalion operated against the FOREST ARGONNE and in conjunction with the infantry took LA FORGE FERME (02.6-75.3) and MONTBLAINVILLE (02.0-75.7).

Lieutenants Higgins, Llewellyn, and Gibbs with 15 tanks reported from detached service for duty.

DATE: September 28, 1918
ORGANIZATION: 344th Battalion, Companies "A" and "C"
FROM: Very **TO:** Serieux Ferme **DISTANCE:** 4 kilometers
ORGANIZATION: 345th Battalion, Companies "B" and "C"
FROM: Charpentry **TO:** Esperance Ferme
DISTANCE: 2.5 kilometers
ORGANIZATION: 344th Battalion, Company "B" and 345th Battalion, Company "A"
FROM: Montblainville **TO:** Apremont
DISTANCE: 4 kilometers
AVAILABLE FOR ALL DUTY: 23 Officers and 312 Men
WEATHER: Cloudy **ROADS:** Poor **HEALTH:** Good
CAMP: Poor **LOSSES:** 2 Officers wounded; 5 Men killed and 15 Men wounded
[Notes at left margin of diary page:
"Saturday. Map Foret D'Argonne Verdun A.
Operating with 91st Division Right, 35th Division Center, 28th Division Left."]
NARRATIVE OF OPERATIONS:
Lieutenant Higgins reported with one platoon with the 91st Division as a combat liaison group between the 91st and 35th Divisions.

Captain Barnard with 40 tanks from the "A" and "C", 344th Battalion and "B", 345th Battalion, with "C" Company, 345th Battalion as a support, moved against

BAULNY (02.0-77.3), CHAUDRON (02.4-78.5) and SERIEUX FERME (04.1-78.7) and occupied the ground to the east and to the west of MONTREBEAU WOODS (01.5-79.5). The latter, however, was not taken by the infantry.

BAULNY was taken and ESPERANCE FERME (00.9-78.3). At night, however, the infantry fell back to the BAULNY ridge on the west and to the general line of CHAUDRON and SERIEUX FERME on the east. Tanks at CHARPENTRY, VERY and BAULNY for the night.

The west group of tanks under Lieutenant Brown operated from MONTBLAINVILLE against the FOREST ARGONNE (00.-76) and about noon entered the town of APREMONT (00.2-78.0) as per orders of General Muir.[16]

After cleaning the town no infantry appeared and the tanks fell back to a ravine about 800 meters south of the town. They were being held up by machine gun fire from the FOREST ARGONNE again and the tanks once more operated in that direction and Lieutenant Bowes[17] once more entered the town of APREMONT and then fell back to the infantry.

About sundown the general ordered the infantry to follow the tanks and the town was this time occupied by the tanks accompanied by the infantry. Several tanks were left with the infantry there and the balance of the two companies returned to MONTBLAINVILLE for the night.

The French Groups who were reorganizing after the attack and capture of CHARPENTRY were relieved from further duty as their tanks and personnel were in bad condition. On orders from 1st Army they moved to LOCHERES, north CLERMONT, and southwest of AUBREVILLE.

---

[16] Major General Charles Henry Muir.
[17] Second Lieutenant Edward Bowes.

DATE: September 29, 1918
ORGANIZATION: 344th Battalion, "A" Company
FROM: Esperance Ferme **TO:** Exermont
DISTANCE: 3.5 kilometers
AVAILABLE FOR ALL DUTY: 22 Officers and 292 Men
WEATHER: Cloudy **ROADS:** Poor **HEALTH:** Good
CAMP: Poor **LOSSES:** 4 Men wounded
[Notes at left margin of diary page:
"Sunday. Map Foret D'Argonne Verdun 1/20.
Operating with 91st Division Right, 35th Division Center,
28th Division Left."]
NARRATIVE OF OPERATIONS:

Captain English operating out of BAULNY moved on and entered EXERMONT (01.7-80.9) but without infantry support he was not able to hold it and withdrew after the infantry fell back, and spent the night at his lying-in point at BAULNY.

Some confusion among the infantry on the east near MONTREBEAU (01.5-79.5) caused them to give way some small gains, but the tanks who were waiting for orders were sent in by Captain Barnard north of CHARPENTRY and by Lieutenant Grant northwest of VERY on orders of Captain Compton and the line settled down to the old position—BAULNY-CHAUDRON-SERIEUX FERME—although somewhat advanced above BAULNY nearer L'ESPERANCE FERME (00.9-78.3). Lying-in points remained the same.

In Lieutenant Brown's groups, Lieutenants Gibbs and Roy attempted to work north out of APREMONT, but the artillery from forward as well as "shorts" from our artillery or perhaps, as also reported a "wild-cat" gun from the ARGONNE FORET, made any operations impossible.

The infantry did nothing and General Nolan held the tanks for a counterattack which the tanks were able to ward off and the Boche withdrew. The line remained the same.

Tank supplies were sent to APREMONT and the two platoons remained with General Nolan during the night.

The balance of the two companies remained at
MONTBLAINVILLE.

DATE: September 30, 1918
AVAILABLE FOR ALL DUTY: 22 Officers and 288 Men
WEATHER: Rain **ROADS:** Poor **HEALTH:** Good
CAMP: Poor **LOSSES:** [3 or 0] Men wounded [numbers
written over each other]
[Notes at left margin of diary page:
"Monday. Map Foret D'Argonne Verdun 1/20.
Operating with 91st Division Right, 35th Division Center,
28th Division Left."]
NARRATIVE OF OPERATIONS:
Tanks were ordered held in reserve and both
Captain English and Lieutenant Grant were ordered to
move to CHARPENTRY (03.2-76.7).

About 8:00 a.m., the 35th Division asked for
assistance for a reported Boche attack from northeast
ECLISFONTAINE[18] (05.8-78.9) and 24 tanks were
deployed in position at SERIEUX FERME (04.1-78.8).

No attack developed and the tanks drew
considerable artillery fire and after waiting some four
hours they withdrew to prepare for an attack scheduled
for 2:00 p.m. This order for an attack at 2:00 p.m. on
MONTREBEAU WOODS (01.5-79.5) was rescinded.

At 6:00 p.m. message received that the 1st Division
would relieve the 35th Division in the east sector, and to be
prepared to attack with them the following day. All east
groups of tanks were consolidated at CHARPENTRY.

Captain Barnard, Captain English, Lieutenant Phillips
and Lieutenant Grant in command of Company "C," 345th
Battalion, Company "C," 344th Battalion, Company "B,"

---

[18] "The 91st Division, on the first day's advance had pierced the Volker
Stellung and on the 27th progressed against Epinonville and Eclisfontaine and
while it suffered heavy casualties from machine guns on its front and flanks, and
especially on its left flank where it was completely out of touch with the 35th
Division, it continued the advance until the front rested on the Eclisfontaine
road." Thomas, p. 249.

345th Battalion and Company "A," 344th Battalion, respectively.

In the west sector Lieutenant Heitz[19] was in command of the two platoons held at APREMONT (00.2-78.0) but no attack developed and General Nolan only held them in readiness. The tanks remained at APREMONT during the night. MONTBLAINVILLE (02.0-75.7) remained the command post of this group. A patrol went out of APREMONT in the afternoon.

---

[19] Second Lieutenant Harry D. Heitz.

COMPTON WAR DIARY - OCTOBER 1918

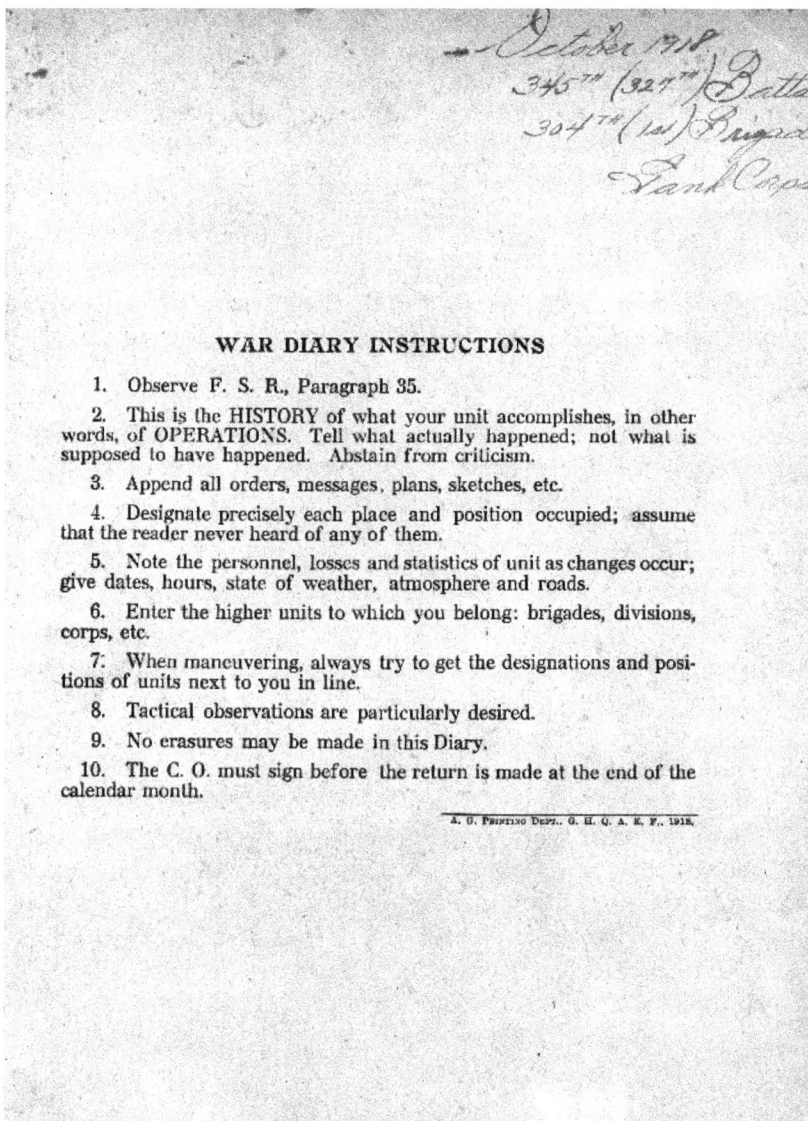

October 1918
345th (327th) Batta.
304th (1st) Brigade
Tank Corps

WAR DIARY INSTRUCTIONS

1. Observe F. S. R., Paragraph 35.

2. This is the HISTORY of what your unit accomplishes, in other words, of OPERATIONS. Tell what actually happened; not what is supposed to have happened. Abstain from criticism.

3. Append all orders, messages, plans, sketches, etc.

4. Designate precisely each place and position occupied; assume that the reader never heard of any of them.

5. Note the personnel, losses and statistics of unit as changes occur; give dates, hours, state of weather, atmosphere and roads.

6. Enter the higher units to which you belong: brigades, divisions, corps, etc.

7. When maneuvering, always try to get the designations and positions of units next to you in line.

8. Tactical observations are particularly desired.

9. No erasures may be made in this Diary.

10. The C. O. must sign before the return is made at the end of the calendar month.

A. G. PRINTING DEPT., G. H. Q. A. E. F., 1918.

Image of cover to Compton's War Diary for October 1918.

DATE: October 1, 1918
AVAILABLE FOR ALL DUTY: 23 Officers and 288 Men
WEATHER: Cloudy **ROADS:** Fair **HEALTH:** Good
CAMP: Fair **LOSSES:** 1 Man killed and 13 Men wounded
[Notes at left margin of diary page:
"Tuesday. Map Foret D'Argonne Verdun 1/20.
Operating with 91st Division Right, 1st Division Center,
28th Division Left."]

NARRATIVE OF OPERATIONS:

The east group under Captain Barnard was held in reserve and had no action. The opportunity was embraced to give considerable attention to making repairs, etc., in spite of a continuous enemy shell fire. Each night the little valley near CHARPENTRY (03.2-76.7) was freely gassed but the tanks remained.

At APREMONT (00.2-78.0) a very stiff Boche attack developed. Lieutenant Heitz with Lieutenant Louiselle[1] and two platoons immediately went out in front of the town to meet it. There is no question but that Lieutenant Heitz's prompt action and subsequent determined resistance turned the Boche attack into a small rout. General Nolan personally complimented him on his services.

The seriousness of the attack is proved by the heavy casualties. Sergeant Dutt and Corporal Whitney and Private First Class Casey were killed and others were seriously wounded. Five tanks were completely wrecked by heavy artillery fire.

Prisoners captured by the infantry, including two officers and 36 men, when questioned by the intelligence officer of the 28th Division reported "that the tanks treated them just like ironing clothes. They passed through their lines, turned and ran over them. They never had any experience with tanks."

---

[1] Spelled Louisell in manning roster titled, "Condition of Provisional Company, 1st Brigade. Officers Present," p. 48.

Lieutenant Heitz's own tank was struck and wrecked by a large projectile, but both he and his driver escaped without serious injury. Lieutenant Brown's command post remained at MONTBLAINVILLE (02.0-75.7).

DATE: October 2, 1918
AVAILABLE FOR ALL DUTY: 22 Officers and 274 Men
WEATHER: Rain **ROADS:** Fair **HEALTH:** Good **CAMP:** Fair
[Notes at left margin of diary page:
"Wednesday. Map Foret D'Argonne Verdun 1/20.
Operating with 91st Division Right,
1st Division Center, 28th Division Left."]
NARRATIVE OF OPERATIONS:
Lieutenants Saul and Kelley[2] made the most of the inactivity in both sectors by doing all that was possible to put the tanks in battle or running condition. They and the battalion repair units literally worked night and day at both CHARPENTRY (03.2-76.7) and MONTBLAINVILLE (02.0-75.7) as well as in the field.

The east sector was again quiet.

Both Lieutenant Heitz and Lieutenant Louiselle were relieved. Two platoons, tanks and crews went in with Lieutenants Roy and Bowes. Lieutenant Winters[3] was wounded and evacuated.

DATE: October 3, 1918
AVAILABLE FOR ALL DUTY: 22 Officers and 274 Men
WEATHER: Cloudy **ROADS:** Fair **HEALTH:** Good
CAMP: Fair **LOSSES:** 1 Man wounded
[Notes at left margin of diary page:
"Thursday. Map Foret D'Argonne Verdun 1/20.
Operating with 91st Division Right, 1st Division Center,
28th Division Left."]
NARRATIVE OF OPERATIONS:
In contemplation of a corps attack the following morning there was no work outlined for either sector. The Boche

---

[2] Second Lieutenant Aloysius J. Kelley, Tank Corps.
[3] First Lieutenant Fred C. Winters, Tank Corps.

apparently was quite willing to take a rest, for he made no attack and only continued his artillery activity.

The 5th Corps and 1st and 28th Division orders for the attack were issued in the early afternoon. Instead of the usual round of inspection, Captain Compton called a conference at each of the respective command posts and with all officers in the sector present the problem was very carefully studied.

The 1st Division order was particularly comprehensive and at Captain Compton's request they very promptly furnished sufficient prepared maps to supply all officers needing them. It is worthy of comment that the tank brigade found the work with the 1st Division, both the staff and the officers and men in the field, most satisfactory.

Detailed report of the condition of the tanks and the personnel as well as a general reorganization was made during the day.

All command posts in the brigade remained the same.

DATE: October 4, 1918
ORGANIZATION: 344th Battalion, Companies "A" and "C" and 345th Battalion, Companies "B" and "C"
FROM: Baulny-Serieux Ferme **TO:** Fleville-Cote 240
DISTANCE: 5 kilometers
ORGANIZATION: 344th Battalion, Company "B" and 345th Battalion, Company "A"
FROM: Apremont **TO:** Chatel Chehery
DISTANCE: 3 kilometers
AVAILABLE FOR ALL DUTY: 22 Officers and 273 Men
WEATHER: Cloudy **ROADS:** Fair **HEALTH:** Good
CAMP: Fair **LOSSES:** 3 Officers wounded; 3 Men killed and 8 Men wounded
[Notes at left margin of diary page:
"Friday. Map Foret D'Argonne Verdun 1/20.
Operating with 32nd Division Right, 1st Division Center, 28th Division Left, 77th Division Left."]
NARRATIVE OF OPERATIONS:
At 5:30 a.m. the attack began in face of very determined resistance. The line in the east sector advanced and took

MONTREBEAU WOODS (01.5-79.5), EXERMONT (01.7-80.9), CHEHERY (99.1-80.4) and dug in several hundred meters north of EXERMONT where they threatened COTE 240 and 212.

The tanks went to FLEVILLE (99-82) but the infantry could not make it on account of the heavy fire from the west side of the AIRE RIVER. There were fifty tanks engaged in this sector. The loss was heavy in tanks.

Captain English, Lieutenant Llewellyn and four enlisted men were killed, while Lieutenants Phillips, Gleason, Wood, Sewall, Morrison, McCluer and Nelms were wounded with many casualties among the [enlisted] men.

In the west sector 16 tanks operated. Lieutenants Roy and Bowes especially did good work with their platoons in advance of the infantry, which took and occupied LA FORGE (98.8-79.8) and CHATEL CHEHERY (97.8-79.5).

Lieutenant Gibbs with one platoon operated near LE CHENE TONDU (99.5-76.8), but four of his tanks were put out of commission. The enemy artillery set up in the forest in addition to literally hundreds of machine guns has made the taking of LE CHENE TONDU a most difficult problem for both tanks and infantry. Some progress was made, however.

All command posts remained the same.

DATE: October 5, 1918
ORGANIZATION: 345th Battalion, Company "A"
FROM: Chatel Chehery **TO:** Near Cote 180
DISTANCE: 2.5 kilometers
AVAILABLE FOR ALL DUTY: 19 Officers and 262 Men
WEATHER: Cloudy **ROADS:** Fair **HEALTH:** Good
CAMP: Fair
[Notes at left margin of diary page:
"Saturday. Map Foret D'Argonne Verdun 1/20.
Operating with 32nd Division Right, 1st Division Center,
28th Division Left, 77th Division Left."]

NARRATIVE OF OPERATIONS:

Lieutenant Gibbs with the infantry again attempted to take LE CHENE TONDU (99.5-76.8), but the resistance of artillery, machine guns, liquid fire, trench mortars, anti-tank guns and continued Boche counterattacks made only a slight gain of 50 meters possible. Lieutenant Louiselle did some patrolling in the neighborhood of the RIVER AIRE and LA FORGE (98.8-79.8).

In the east sector the tanks and personnel were in such a condition that further operations at the moment were impossible. The continued use of gas by the enemy caused many evacuations.

All tanks disabled were ordered brought in to the lying-in point at CHARPENTRY (03.2-76.7) for repair if possible.

All command posts remained the same.

DATE: October 6, 1918
AVAILABLE FOR ALL DUTY: 19 Officers and 262 Men
WEATHER: Rain **ROADS:** Good **HEALTH:** Good
CAMP: Fair **LOSSES:** 2 Officers wounded; 24 Men wounded
[Notes at left margin of diary page:
"Sunday. Map Foret D'Argonne Verdun 1/20.
Operating with 32nd Division Right, 1st Division Center,
28th Division Left, 77th Division Left."]

NARRATIVE OF OPERATIONS:

This day was given up to such reorganization as was possible. The tanks were in bad condition generally as under the conditions it had been impossible to do any overhauling, carbon scraping, and other necessary mechanical work to keep motors and machinery running.

There was not a single tank in first class battle condition, since all tanks had been used constantly as fast as hurried repairs could get them running again. Certain tanks were turned over to the Repair and Salvage Company at Varennes (03.5-73.4).

About two platoons on each side of the river, that is, in each sector, were held in readiness for an emergency call.

DATE: October 7, 1918
AVAILABLE FOR ALL DUTY: 17 Officers and 238 Men
WEATHER: Rain **ROADS:** Good **HEALTH:** Good
CAMP: Fair **LOSSES:** 2 Men killed and 1 Man wounded
[Notes at left margin of diary page:
"Monday. Map Foret D'Argonne Verdun.
Operating with 32nd Division Right, 1st Division Center,
28th Division Left, 77th Division Left."]

NARRATIVE OF OPERATIONS:

The tanks attempted to join the attack in both sectors, but all broke down in moving forward and none were able to get in. Their only result was the excellent moral effect upon our own infantry.

In the east sector eight tanks were sent up, one struck a mine and was disabled and the rest managed to report, but were not used.

DATE: October 8, 1918
AVAILABLE FOR ALL DUTY: 17 Officers and 235 Men
WEATHER: Rain **ROADS:** Good **HEALTH:** Fair **CAMP:** Fair
LOSSES: 2 Men wounded
[Notes at left margin of diary page:
"Tuesday. Map Foret D'Argonne Verdun 1/20.
Operating with 32nd Division Right, 1st Division Center,
28th Division Left, 82nd Division Left, 77th Division Left."]

NARRATIVE OF OPERATIONS:

Further attempts were made to get forward with tanks, but without any success due to their bad mechanical condition.

Twenty-six tanks were in running condition and constituted a reserve for both sectors. They were not called for, however.

DATE: October 9, 1918
AVAILABLE FOR ALL DUTY: 17 Officers and 233 Men
WEATHER: Rain **ROADS:** Good **HEALTH:** Fair **CAMP:** Fair
LOSSES: 1 Officer wounded; 4 Men wounded
[Notes at left margin of diary page:
"Wednesday. Map Foret D'Argonne Verdun 1/20.
Operating with 32nd Division Right, 1st Division Center,
28th Division Left, 82nd Division Left, 77th Division Left."]

NARRATIVE OF OPERATIONS:

It was impossible to get the tanks, such was their mechanical condition, to the front. Even when a single tank did arrive now and then it was manifestly unfit for battle. This added to the apprehension of the crews already near the end of their endurance.

In spite of the conditions both officers and men continued to work on the tanks and tried with all their wits and strength to get them into battle, but without availing anything.

Captain Compton moved his command post to MONTBLAINVILLE (02.0-75.7) near the command post of the west group. Major Brett moved his command post to VARENNES (03.5-73.4); CHARPENTRY (03.2-76.7) remained.

The tanks in running condition stood by during the day but were not called for. All personnel engaged in making repairs.

DATE: October 10, 1918
AVAILABLE FOR ALL DUTY: 10 Officers and 229 Men
WEATHER: Cloudy **ROADS:** Good **HEALTH:** Fair
CAMP: Fair
[Notes at left margin of diary page:
"Thursday. Map Foret D'Argonne Verdun 1/20.
Operating with 32nd Division Right, 1st Division Center,
77th Division Left, 82nd Division Left."]

NARRATIVE OF OPERATIONS:

All personnel, both combatant and mechanical, were put on the two companies of tanks, which were given special mechanical attention with a view of putting entirely fresh crews to man them assisting in an attack on the morning of the 11th, north of FLEVILLE (99-82). Lieutenant Rattray,[4] who had been doing liaison duty and was anxious for the assignment, was picked to command the leading platoon.

At the same time 25 tanks in the repair and salvage park in various states of hurried repair were ordered to leave at dark for the front.

In accordance with these instructions they started under Captain Barnard. Captain Compton was gassed during the night of October 9th-10th. Although requiring medical attention, he continued in command.

Captain Barnard reported to Captain Compton about midnight that the tanks were on the road but making poor progress.

DATE: October 11, 1918
ORGANIZATION: 345th Battalion, Company "C"
FROM: Varennes **TO:** Fleville **DISTANCE:** 12 kilometers
AVAILABLE FOR ALL DUTY: 10 Officers and 203 Men
WEATHER: Cloudy **ROADS:** Good **HEALTH:** Fair
CAMP: Fair

[Notes at left margin of diary page:
"Friday. Map Foret D'Argonne Verdun 1/20.
Operating with 32nd Division Right, 1st Division Center,
77th Division Left, 82nd Division Left."]

NARRATIVE OF OPERATIONS:

Only four tanks in all reached FLEVILLE (99-82) ready for the attack. These were under Lieutenant Rattray. Two of these broke down entering the attack and under orders from Chief of Tank Corps that no less than a platoon should operate; the attack as far as the tanks were concerned was abandoned.

The group at CHARPENTRY were ordered to assemble all tanks, supplies and personnel at VARENNES. Lieutenant Brown was able to assemble four tanks at 96.7-78.8 in the west sector in the early morning, but they were not called for by the infantry who were to put them in if needed and

---

[4] Second Lieutenant Walter Rattray.

Lieutenant Brown was ordered to assemble his group at VARENNES at nightfall.

DATE: October 12, 1918
AVAILABLE FOR ALL DUTY: 10 Officers and 196 Men
WEATHER: Rain **ROADS:** Good **CAMP:** Fair
[Notes at left margin of diary page:
"Saturday. Map Foret D'Argonne Verdun 1/20.
Operating with 32nd Division Right, 1st Division Center,
77th Division Left, 82nd Division Left."]

NARRATIVE OF OPERATIONS:

Both groups reported with all tanks and personnel at VARENNES and Captain Compton was relieved by Major Brett of the command of the forward tanks and again took command of the 345th Battalion. The battalion operations for the present were finished.

It is here pertinent to comment on the excellent and continuous work of the supply officers, Lieutenant Struyk and Lieutenant King, who under the direction of Captain Compton, had furnished the brigade at all times with a full supply of rations, gas, oil, and ammunition.

The painstaking care and high professional skill of the medical detachments under Lieutenant A. Isom, M.C. of the 345th Battalion and as well as Lieutenant L. H. Howard, M.C.[5] of the 344th Battalion, proved never-failing. Every attention was given to the Tank Corps personnel as well as aiding at all times all other wounded.

DATE: October 13, 1918
AVAILABLE FOR ALL DUTY: 10 Officers and 196 Men
WEATHER: Rain **ROADS:** Good **CAMP:** Fair
[Notes at left margin of diary page:
"Sunday. Map Foret D'Argonne Verdun 1/20.
Operating with 32nd Division Right, 1st Division Center,
77th Division Left, 82nd Division Left."]

---

[5] First Lieutenant Lewis H. Howard, M.D.

NARRATIVE OF OPERATIONS:

The 345th Battalion started to move by truck and automobile to BOURG, turning over all tanks, and tank material to Major Brett, and leaving a detachment from the battalion to make up part of the composite company to remain with the tanks.

DATE: October 14, 1918
AVAILABLE FOR ALL DUTY: 9 Officers and 90 Men
WEATHER: Rain **ROADS:** Good **CAMP:** Fair

NARRATIVE OF OPERATIONS:

The 345th Battalion reached BOURG and was detached from the 304th Brigade (formerly the 1st Brigade) and assigned to the 306th Brigade. Captain Compton reported to the Brigade Commander, Colonel D. D. Pullen at BRENNES.

DATE: October 15, 1918
AVAILABLE FOR ALL DUTY: 11 Officers and 87 Men
CAMP: Fair

NARRATIVE OF OPERATIONS:

The battalion engaged in putting barracks in good condition and fatigue duty only.

DATE: October 16, 1918
AVAILABLE FOR ALL DUTY: 11 Officers and 87 Men
CAMP: Fair

NARRATIVE OF OPERATIONS:

Fatigue duty, including building mess tables, kitchen shelving and so forth.

The men gave attention to personal bathing and washing clothes.

DATE: October 17, 1918
AVAILABLE FOR ALL DUTY: 10 Officers and 87 Men
CAMP: Fair

NARRATIVE OF OPERATIONS:

Fatigue duty only.

DATE: October 18, 1918
AVAILABLE FOR ALL DUTY: 10 Officers and 87 Men
NARRATIVE OF OPERATIONS:
Fatigue and clothing issue.

DATE: October 19, 1918
AVAILABLE FOR ALL DUTY: 10 Officers and 349 Men
NARRATIVE OF OPERATIONS:
Company inspection and inspection of quarters and kitchens.

DATE: October 20, 1918
AVAILABLE FOR ALL DUTY: 10 Officers and 349 Men
NARRATIVE OF OPERATIONS:
No regular duty.

DATE: October 21, 1918
AVAILABLE FOR ALL DUTY: 10 Officers and 349 Men
NARRATIVE OF OPERATIONS:
Drill, instruction and fatigue.

DATE: October 22, 1918
AVAILABLE FOR ALL DUTY: 10 Officers and 349 Men
NARRATIVE OF OPERATIONS:
Drill, instruction and fatigue.

DATE: October 23, 1918
AVAILABLE FOR ALL DUTY: [? - Uncertain. Appears to be the number 1 crossed through] Officers and 349 Men
NARRATIVE OF OPERATIONS:
Drill, instruction and fatigue.

DATE: October 24, 1918
AVAILABLE FOR ALL DUTY: 349 Men
NARRATIVE OF OPERATIONS:
Drill, instruction and fatigue.

DATE: October 25, 1918
AVAILABLE FOR ALL DUTY: 349 Men

NARRATIVE OF OPERATIONS:
Drill, instruction and fatigue.

DATE: October 26, 1918
AVAILABLE FOR ALL DUTY: 349 Men
NARRATIVE OF OPERATIONS:
Battalion inspection in a.m.

DATE: October 27, 1918
AVAILABLE FOR ALL DUTY: 349 Men
NARRATIVE OF OPERATIONS:
No duty.

DATE: October 28, 1918
AVAILABLE FOR ALL DUTY: 349 Men
NARRATIVE OF OPERATIONS:
Lectures by Company Commanders, drill instruction and fatigue.

DATE: October 29, 1918
AVAILABLE FOR ALL DUTY: 349 Men
NARRATIVE OF OPERATIONS:
Lecture by Battalion Commander. Company drill and instruction.

DATE: October 30, 1918
AVAILABLE FOR ALL DUTY: [Left blank.]
NARRATIVE OF OPERATIONS:
Lecture by Battalion Commander. Company drill and instruction.

DATE: October 31, 1918
AVAILABLE FOR ALL DUTY: 24 Officers and 357 Men
NARRATIVE OF OPERATIONS:
Lecture by Battalion Commander. Company drill and instruction.

BIBLIOGRAPHY

Abbott, Willis J. <u>The United States in the Great War</u>. New
    York: Leslie-Judge Co., 1919.

Allison, J. Murray. <u>Raemaekers' Cartoon History of the War</u>.
    New York: The Century Co., 1918.

Blumenson, Martin. <u>Patton: The Man Behind the Legend,</u>
    <u>1885-1945</u>. New York: Quill - William Morrow, 1985.

_____. <u>The Patton Papers 1885-1940</u>. Boston: Houghton
    Mifflin Company, 1972.

Boraston, J.H. <u>Sir Douglas Haig's Despatches</u>. London &
    Toronto: J.M. Dent & Sons LTD, 1919.

Buchan, John. <u>A History of the Great War</u>. Vols. I-IV.
    Boston: Houghton Mifflin Company, 1923.

Cotton, Robert C. "A Study of the St. Mihiel Offensive,"
    <u>Infantry Journal</u>. XVII, No. 1 (July 1920), 43-59.

D'Este, Carlo. <u>Patton: A Genius for War</u>. New York:
    HarperPerennial, 1996.

Doyle, Arthur Conan. <u>A History of the Great War: The</u>
    <u>British Campaign in France and Flanders 1918 July</u>
    <u>to November</u>. Vol. Six. New York: George H. Doran
    Company, 1920.

Egan, Maurice F. <u>A Brief History of the Great War</u>. New
    York: William H. Sadlier, 1919.

Eisenhower, D. D. "A Tank Discussion," <u>Infantry Journal</u>.
    XVII, No. 5 (November 1920), 453-458.

Farago, Ladislas. <u>Patton: Ordeal and Triumph</u>. New York:
    Ivan Obolensky, Inc., 1964.

<u>Field Service Regulations United States Army 1914</u>,
    Corrected to July 31, 1918. Washington, D.C.:
    Government Printing Office, 1918.

Hirshson, Stanley P. <u>General Patton: A Soldier's Life</u>. New
    York: Perennial, 2003.

Horne, Charles F. Ph.D. and Walter F. Austin, LL.M., eds.
    <u>The Great Events of the Great War</u>. Vol. VI. The
    National Alumni, 1920.

List, Major Single. "The Battle of Booby's Bluffs." <u>Infantry</u>
    <u>Journal</u>. Published in six installments: XVIII, No. 5
    (May 1921), 447-458; XVIII, No. 6 (June 1921), 606-
    611; XIX, No. 1 (July 1921), 41-50; XIX, No. 2

(August 1921), 149-155; XIX, No. 3 (September 1921), 295-302; and XIX, No. 4 (October 1921), 427-433. Verbatim transcription published by same title, The Battle of Booby's Bluffs. Silver Spring: Dale Street Books, 2017.

Ludendorff, General. My War Memories. Vols. I and II. London: Hutchinson & Co., 1919.

McKinley, Albert E., Charles A. Coulomb, and Armand J. Gerson. A School History of the Great War. New York: American Book Company, 1918.

Order of Battle of the United States Land Forces in the World War. Vol. 1. American Expeditionary Forces: General Headquarters, Armies, Army Corps, Services of Supply, Separate Forces. Washington, D.C.: Center of Military History United States Army, 1988.

Order of Battle of the United States Land Forces in the World War. Vol. 2. American Expeditionary Forces: Divisions. Washington, D.C.: Center of Military History United States Army, 1988.

Order of Battle of the United States Land Forces in the World War (1917-1919). Vol. Three, Part 1. General Introduction, Organization and Activities of the War Department, Territorial Departments, Tactical Divisions Organized in 1918, Posts, Camps, and Stations. Washington, D.C.: World War I Group, Historical Division Special Staff United States Army, 1949.

Order of Battle of the United States Land Forces in the World War (1917-1919). Vol. Three, Part 2. Directory of Troops in Alphabetical Order. Washington, D.C.: World War I Group, Historical Division Special Staff United States Army, 1949.

Palmer, Frederick. America in France. New York: Dodd, Mead and Company, 1918.

_____. Our Greatest Battle. New York: Dodd, Mead and Company, 1919.

Patton, George S., Jr. "304th American Brigade at St. Mihiel: Operations of the 304th Tank Brigade, September 12th to 15th, 1918," November 12, 1918. Appendix 4, U.S. Army Expeditionary Force, France, 1917-1919, Tank Corps: Report Operations Tank Corps, A.E.F.

BIBLIOGRAPHY

France: General HQs A.E.F., Office of Chief of Tank
Corps, 1918. Carlisle: U.S. Army Heritage and
Education Center, Ridgway Hall, D608.U56 1918.

_____. "Tanks in Future Wars," Infantry Journal. XVI,
No. 11 (May 1920), 958-962.

Pershing, John J. My Experiences in the World War. Vols. I
and II. New York: Frederick A. Stokes Company,
1931.

Punch Magazine. Mr. Punch's History of the Great War. New
York: Frederick A. Stokes Company, 1919.

Rockenbach, Samuel D. Operations of the Tank Corps,
A.E.F. Silver Spring: Dale Street Books, 2017.
Verbatim transcription of unpublished document
commonly known as the Rockenbach Report, dated
November 1918.

_____. "Tanks and their Cooperation with other Arms,"
Infantry Journal. Published in installments: XVI, No.
7 (January 1920), 533-545; XVI, No. 8 (February
1920), 662-673.

_____. U.S. Army Expeditionary Force, France, 1917-
1919, Tank Corps: Report Operations Tank Corps,
A.E.F. France: General HQs A.E.F., Office of Chief of
Tank Corps, 1918. Carlisle: U.S. Army Heritage and
Education Center, Ridgway Hall, D608.U56 1918.

Rogge, Robert E. "304th Tank Brigade: Its Formation and
First Two Actions," Armor. XCVII, No. 4 (July-August
1988), 26-34.

Simonds, Frank H. History of the World War. Vol. 5. New
York: Doubleday, Page & Company, 1920.

Source Records of the Great War. Vols. I-VII. National
Alumni, 1923.

Stamps, T. Dodson and Vincent J. Esposito. A Short Military
History of World War I.: Atlas. West Point, New York:
Department of Military Art and Engineering, 1950.

Stanton, Theodore, Translator. A Soldier of France to His
Mother. Chicago: A.C. McClurg & Co., 1917.

The Americans in the Great War. Vol. I. The Second Battle of
the Marne (Chateau-Thierry, Soissons, Fismes).
France: Michelin & Cie, Clermont-Ferrand, 1919.

The Americans in the Great War. Vol. II. The Battle of St. Mihiel (St. Mihiel, Pont-a-Mousson, Metz). France: Michelin & Cie, Clermont-Ferrand, 1920.

The Americans in the Great War. Vol. III. Meuse-Argonne Battlefields (Montfaucon, Romagne, Sainte-Menehould). France: Michelin & Cie, Clermont-Ferrand, 1920.

The Story of the Great War. Vol. XV. New York: P.F. Collier & Son, 1920.

Thomas, Shipley. The History of the A.E.F. New York: George H. Doran Company, 1920.

Von Giehrl, Hermann. Battle of the Meuse-Argonne from the German Perspective. Silver Spring: Dale Street Books, 2017. Reproduction of articles titled "Battle of the Meuse-Argonne," published in installments in the Infantry Journal: Vol. XIX, No. 2 (August 1921), 131-138; Vol. XIX, No. 3 (September 1921), 264-270; Vol. XIX, No. 4 (October 1921), 377-384; and Vol. XIX, No. 5 (November 1921), 534-540.

_____. *Das Amerikanische Expeditionskorps in Europa 1917–18.* Originally published as an article in the German Military Journal, *Wissen und Wehr* (July 1921), pp. 217-340. Also published independently under same title by Berlin: E.S. Mittler & Sohn, 1922.

_____. The American Expeditionary Forces in Europe, 1917-1918. Silver Spring: Dale Street Books, 2018. Reproduction of English translation of *Das Amerikanische Expeditionskorps in Europa 1917–18*, published by the Infantry Journal in installments: Vol. XIX, No. 6 (December 1921), 630-637; Vol. XX, No. 1 (January 1922), 18-23; Vol. XX, No. 2 (February 1922), 140-149; and Vol. XX, No. 3 (March 1922), pp. 292-303.

Wilson, Dale E. Treat 'Em Rough: The Birth of American Armor, 1917-20. Novato, California: Presidio Press, 1990.

INDEX

INDEX

INDEX

Renault (Light) Tank (see also "Tanks"), xxiv, 13, 42, 71, 72.

Repair and Salvage, 6, 28, 32, 40, 42, 52, 53, 55, 57, 60, 64, 65, 102; Repair and Salvage Company redesignated from 316th to 321st, 9; repairs becoming more difficult, 32, 98; evacuating disabled tanks, 39, 40; repair park, 39, 55, 105; hurried repairs, 99, 102, 105.

Roberts, Harold W.—Killed in action, 60; cited for heroism, 60.

Rockenbach, Samuel D. (see also "Pershing, John J."), vii, 3, 6, 9, 14, 19, 36, 41, 67; Rockenbach Report, vii; Chief, Tank Corps, vii, xxiv, 5; Tank School at Ft. Meade, xxxvi.

Roy, John W., 29, 94, 99, 101.

Runners (see "Communications, Modes of").

Rupt de Mad River, 5.

Sandford (see also "Lulworth"), 54, 59.

Saul, Tom W., 79, 99.

Schneider Assault Tank (see also "Tanks"), 17, 18, 87.

Semmes, Harry Hodges, 5; cited for heroism, 60, 61; wounded, 88, 89.

Serieux Ferme, 28, 29, 35, 92-95, 100.

Sewall, Loyall F.—Wounded, 36, 101.

Sickness among troops, 39.

South Hampton, 62.

St. Benoit, 80.

St. Chamond Heavy Tank (see also "Tanks"), 17.

St. Georges, 53, 64.

St. Maurice, 12.

St. Mihiel Salient, v, vii, xxviii; rushing to Argonne, xxxiii, preparing for, 8, 9, 74; battle of 10-12, 77-81; commendations, 15, 16, 18, 19.

Struyk, Gus, 81, 106.

Summerall, C. P. (see also "1st Division"), 16.

Tanks—Entry into war, vii; with 37mm guns, xxiii, 44, 70, 72; with machine guns, xxiii, 44, 70, 72; demoralizing effect on enemy, 18, 19, 32, 37, 98; mechanical issues, 36, 37, 40, 41, 99; poor condition 38, 79, 102-104; rejected, 41; unaccounted for 56, 57, 58.

Tank Corps, First Army, vi, xxiii, xxvi, xxxii, 4-6, 14, 75, 83, 91, 105, 106; Rockenbach Report, vii, xv, xvii; Rockenbach appointed Chief, Tank Corps, xxiv; redesignation of units, 9, 10; allotment of troops post St. Mihiel, 17; temporary officer appointments, 33, 35; provisional organization, 40-42, 55; units relieved from duty, 57; tanks requested for operations, 58;

121

Other Publications from

DALE STREET BOOKS

Military Strategy, Tactics and Training

Battle of Booby's Bluffs is a blunt depiction of incompetence by some American Army officers in World War I, who were unable to adapt their old-fashioned tactics to the new weapons of modern war–tanks, machine guns, stokes mortars, and airplanes. Written in the dream-sequence style of the infantry classic, <u>Defence of Duffer's Drift</u>, the main character is a pompous know-it-all who relives the same dream over and over until by trial and error he learns how to keep his men alive and win on the modern battlefield. Written under the pseudonym Major Single List, the anonymous author had good reason to hide his identity, given the number of feathers his amusing but highly critical book likely ruffled.

Cavalry and Tanks in Future Wars is a collection of articles written by George S. Patton, in which he applies his diverse experiences as a cavalry officer chasing Pancho Villa on the Mexican Border and a tank commander on the battlefields in 1918 France to defend the continued relevance of cavalry and tanks in future wars.

Diary of the Instructor in Swordsmanship is the second training manual written by George S. Patton, Jr., to teach cavalry officers the proper saber tactics and techniques for mounted and dismounted engagements. (His first training manual, <u>Saber Exercise 1914</u>, covered the general rules while this second manual presents more detailed instructions.)

In Defense of My Saber is a collection of articles written by George S. Patton, Jr. extolling the virtues of his redesigned cavalry saber. It begins in the glory days when his saber was embraced by the Army as standard issue. It ends with its ultimate decline into irrelevance after the Great War— and despite Patton's ardent pleas to the contrary.

Saber Exercise 1914 Training Manual in Swordsmanship (originally titled <u>Saber Exercise 1914</u>) was written by George S. Patton, Jr. the year after the War Department approved his radical redesign of the cavalry saber. The redesign necessitated a fundamental change in mounted and dismounted saber work—all of which is explained in this manual.

The Defence of Duffer's Drift by Sir Ernest D. Swinton is a classic in the art of infantry tactics and required reading at many Army schools.

World War I in Europe

Battle of the Meuse-Argonne from the German Perspective, by German Army Major Hermann von Giehrl, is a military analysis of the Battle of the Meuse-Argonne from the German point of view. In Major von Giehrl's eyes, the Americans and French are the enemy. But his writing is surprisingly free of nationalistic fervor. Instead he offers an objective view of the 42 days leading up to the German surrender, written by a soldier, not a politician or apologist. Von Giehrl is candid in his assessment of the effectiveness of the French and Germans, traumatized by four long years of the modern battlefield overwhelmed by tanks, aeroplanes, machine guns, mortars and gas. By contrast, his description of the naïve but strapping young Americans as they arrived on a ravaged continent not yet having learned to fear the horrors that awaited them is truly poignant.

The American Expeditionary Forces in Europe 1917-1918, the follow-on analysis of American involvement in the Great War by Hermann von Giehrl of the German Army, was originally published in 1922 in the <u>U.S. Infantry Journal</u>. Von Giehrl was not only a German staff officer but also an excellent writer who was therefore able to capture not only the relevant military analysis but also the human courage and sacrifice in combat.

Operations of the Tank Corps A.E.F. is the official report of the U.S. Army Tank Corps–how it was organized, equipped, manned, trained and then deployed into battle in 1918 France. Commonly known as the Rockenbach Report, it

was compiled by Brigadier General Samuel D.
Rockenbach, the father of the Tank Corps and its first
Commander. Among the addendums to the main report
are an organization roster listing the units and personnel
by name assigned to the Tank Corps in September 1918;
and an operations report by Lieutenant Colonel George S.
Patton, Jr., Commander of 304th Tank Brigade, on the
Battle of St. Mihiel.

War Diary 1918, by George S. Patton, Jr. and Ranulf Compton,
is the verbatim transcript of the original—and only
copies—of the handwritten daily diaries required by the
War Department to be kept by all commanders during the
Great War. It contains the complete and unedited entries
for the 304th (1st Provisional) Tank Brigade of the
American Expeditionary Forces, personally signed by
Patton for each day's entry. It covers three critical
months–from September when Patton's brigade was
preparing to enter combat (first at the Battle of St. Mihiel
and then the Meuse-Argonne Offensive) to the final days
leading up to the Armistice in November. Also included is
the War Diary kept by Captain Ranulf Compton, one of
Patton's battalion commanders, who commanded the
forwarded units of Patton's brigade after Patton was
wounded. Captain Compton's diary entries begin in the
middle of August, as his battalion prepares for combat
and continues through October, offering a detailed and
personal report of the tank battles from the front lines
during some of the toughest fighting of the war. Together
these diaries offer a unique view of the Tank Corps
Brigade—and its forward units—in the critical months of
the Great War, when our boys—and their tanks—turned
the tide of history.

World War II in Europe

Campaign in Poland 1939 is a previously classified analysis by
U.S. military strategists at the Department of Military Art
and Engineering, United States Military Academy,
detailing the "Polish Campaign" instigated by the German
invasion in September 1939. Included are maps showing
the troop movements and engagements over the course of

the four-week conflict that ended with a conquered Poland.

The German Fifth Column in Poland by the Polish Ministry of Information exposes the treachery of the German population living inside Polish borders but lending clandestine assistance to the invading German Army in September 1939.

German Occupation of Poland was published by the Polish Ministry of Foreign Affairs in the first years of the war. It exposed for the first time to the world community the dire conditions in Nazi-occupied Poland with detailed reports on the summary executions of civilians, eviction of Poles from their homes, the closing of schools, synagogues and universities and the forced relocation of Jews into ghettoes.

The Mass Extermination of Jews in German Occupied Poland was written by the Polish Ministry of Foreign Affairs as a plea to the world community to save Polish Jews from the Nazis.

Trying to Stop a War in 1939 showcases the earnest and increasingly frantic communications exchanged between the political and diplomatic representatives of Great Britain, Poland, Germany and Russia in the year leading up to the German invasion of Poland in September 1939. Originally published by the British Foreign Office as a testament to its extraordinary diplomatic efforts to rein in Hitler's territorial ambitions, this historically important collection of speeches, communiqués, cables, letters, messages and notes has been faithfully reproduced verbatim.

Should Great Britain Go to War--for Czechoslovakia? was written by the Slovak Council in 1937 as "an appeal to British common sense for the sake of World Peace."

Polish Literature

Pan Tadeusz, written by Adam Mickiewicz, is a sweeping ode to Polish history and heritage as seen through the eyes of two warring families and the lovers caught in the middle.

Amateur Radio

Popular series of "Quick Study" books to prepare for the exam at the three levels of Amateur Radio license:

Quick Study for Your Technician Class Amateur Radio License

Quick Study for Your General Class Amateur Radio License

Quick Study for Your Extra Class Amateur Radio License

www.ingramcontent.com/pod-product-compliance
Lightning Source LLC
Chambersburg PA
CBHW071451070426
42452CB00039B/1034